# HORNSEA
# GOLF CLUB
## 1898 — 1998

by
**A. A. CLARKE**

ARTON BOOKS 1998

Published by Arton Books
3 Dominican Walk, Beverley, HU17 0HF,
for and on behalf of
HORNSEA GOLF CLUB Ltd.

*Printed by Clifford Ward & Co.*
*(Bridlington) Ltd.,*
*55 West Street, Bridlington East Yorkshire*
*YO15 3DZ*


ISBN 0 9522163 2 9

# CONTENTS

Page

*Hornsea Clubhouse after extension 1997.*

*Stephen Wright*
*Centenary Captain – Hornsea Golf Club.*

*Mr. J. R. Matthews*
*Captain 1997*

*Mr. H. C. Palmer*
*Captain 1999*

5

*The Board of Directors – Hornsea Golf Club Ltd. 1997/1998.*

6

*Mrs. Sheila Jordan*
*Ladies' Centenary Captain.*

*Mrs. J. L. Muirhead*
*Lady Captain 1997.*

*Mrs. Myra Smith*
*Lady Captain 1999.*

7

## FOREWORD
### by the
### CENTENARY CAPTAIN

The publication of this book marks the beginning of the Centenary of the Hornsea Golf Club. A small group of men met in 1898 to consider the introduction into Hornsea of that little-known game which was to become one of the country's most widely enjoyed sporting and social pursuits. In Hornsea it was to grow from small beginnings in what is now Hall Garth Park, into a club whose membership extends far beyond the town, and whose golf course is a focus for golf throughout the East Riding of Yorkshire. It now enjoys a status as one of the premier courses in Yorkshire, with a newly enlarged clubhouse fit to take it on into its second Century.

For that it owes a debt of gratitude to its founders, its Committee members and Directors, its Officers and staff (paid and unpaid) over the years, its succession of Professionals, and above all to its members.

Among such members is Tony Clarke, the author of this volume, arriving in what was then Humberside as its Deputy Chief Constable in 1977. Since his retirement, he has become well known for research into matters of local history and interest, commencing with his book *The Policemen of Hull.* We are indebted to him for his painstaking research and for his generous gift of time and effort for the Club.

Some of what is in here will be familiar to members, particularly those whose membership goes back to 1927 but to others, and to the wider public, it will add to their knowledge of the Club and indeed of Hornsea. I have known the Club for almost half of its life, joining as a Junior member in 1952 during the Captaincy of the late E. L. (Teddy) Biggs and from 1993 until the eve of the Centenary. I have had the privilege of serving as Chairman, relinquishing that office to take on the honour of Captaincy through the Centenary Year. I do so with pride at the thought of serving a Club which has risen to its present height during its first Century, and with high hopes for its prospects in the second.

Stephen L. Wright — December 1997.

8

## MESSAGE FROM THE CENTENARY CHAIRMAN

Sitting in the Centenary Chair is an awesome experience. After all, what can any committee do that will successfully and appropriately commemorate a hundred years of a golf club to the satisfaction of everyone in that club? My committee set out with three simple goals.

1. To focus on the Hornsea members.
2. To make the year an exciting one.
3. To ensure the year's events were self-financing.

All three goals have been achieved — we have a programme of golfing events that will be the envy of our counterparts in other clubs. Our marquee centred fortnight promises to be lots of fun with the Centenary Medals being the goal of all our talented players.

Money raising efforts throughout the past five years have resulted in our being able to fund all the plans and still have money available for a permanent memento of the first centenary of Hornsea Golf Club.

By the time you receive this book the Centenary Committee will have virtually completed the job. The ball is now passed to each and every one of you. We hope you will enjoy this unique year, treasure the individual gifts and participate in all the fun, pageantry and frolics. After all, it is our privilege to be here at the time, we may not make the next centenary!                          Keith Gorton.

*Keith Gorton Centenary Chairman.*

9

## AUTHOR'S NOTE

I wish to express my sincere appreciation to the many who have helped with the production of this book, particularly Keith Gorton the chairman and other members of the centenary committee and especially to Brian Kirton the club secretary for his ever willing assistance. I should join his name with that of Betty Smith, Ladies' Secretary who has never failed to meet my many requests for information.

My grateful thanks go also to the many, mainly mature members, some sadly no longer with us, who gave their time to reminisce about the club's earlier days and also to those who provided photographs and other material for inclusion in the book. Some of the photographs reproduced are done so by kind permission of the Editor, *Hull Daily Mail*. Extracts of O. S. Map is reproduced by kind permission of the Director of H.M. Ordnance Survey.

Liz Pook, an ex Ladies British champion who was sadly disabled in an accident, very kindly spent a lot of time researching the history of Mary Johnson for me and I thank her most sincerely for those efforts. I would also thank those of Mary's family who gave Liz so much help in her work.

It has been a great pleasure and a privilege to write this account and I hope it will be read with enjoyment by present and future members.

I crave the readers' indulgence for any mistakes, omissions etc., of which I am sure there will be many. They will be entirely my fault and I apologise for them in advance.

Tony Clarke

## Chapter 1
## TEEING OFF AT HORNSEA

The 1890's saw Great Britain at the height of its military, economic and political power. An ageing Queen Victoria ruled over a world wide Empire never before equalled in history, and a population at home where wealth and poverty existed side by side. Leisure activities were increasingly being developed among the more affluent and summer time saw townsfolk travelling in increasing numbers to the seaside beaches. Various sporting pursuits including golf were becoming more popular and a number of clubs had already been established in Yorkshire.

The small town of Hornsea had become both a thriving seaside resort and home to many prosperous businessmen from nearby Hull, since the Hull-Hornsea railway had opened in the middle of the century. This had ensured quick and comfortable transport for both daily commuters and visitors to the sea.

Despite the railway however, the end of the nineteenth century still found carriers with horses plying their trade from Hornsea. Miss Rose Carr had her wagon carrying freight between Hornsea and Hull every Tuesday and Friday and her horse drawn omnibus left the Victoria Inn, Hornsea at 9.15 a.m. every Saturday for Beverley.

It was against this background that a meeting was held in Insurance Manager Mr. Collinson's house at 'Fairfield' Cliff Road, Hornsea on the evening of Wednesday 25th May 1898 to discuss the feasibility of starting a golf club in the town. The meeting was attended by Messrs. Minnett Good, Gregson, Broderick, Maw, Holmes and Dr. Johns, many of whom were subsequently to have their names perpetuated on golfing trophies at Hornsea. Mr. Gregson took the chair at the meeting and Mr. Good was appointed secretary.

It was agreed a club should be formed and discussion turned to land which might be suitable for golf links. Three main possibilities were considered, Rowlston fields, Station fields, and Old Hall fields (sometimes known as Hall Garth).

11

*"Fairfield" Cliff Road scene of the first meeting to discuss formation of a Golf Club at Hornsea in 1898.*

Having decided to pursue the idea no time was lost, the three venues were inspected and Old Hall fields chosen as the best site. An agreement was signed with local farmer Mr. Harker to rent sufficient ground for nine holes at an annual charge of £15. Tom Vardon the well known professional from Ilkley and brother of the current English champion Harry Vardon, was retained to design the course and decided the proposed land was ideal and would only require nine greens to be cut and rolled for an area of 14 square yards each and for them to be wired to keep the sheep away. The card of the new course read:      4; 4; 4; 3; 4; 4; 5; 4; 5; = 37

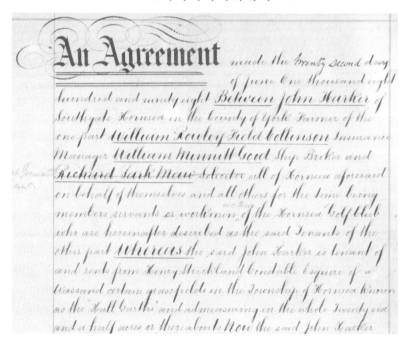

It was decided to ask Captain Frederick Charles S. Constable of Wassand Hall to be the club's first President and Thomas Gregson of Flamborough House, Hornsea was appointed the first Captain. W. Minnett Good of Spring Lawn, Football Green took on the post of Secretary and F. S. Broderick of The Pillars, Westgate was made treasurer. These, together with twenty other members started Hornsea Golf Club. The founder members were;

| | | |
|---|---|---|
| J. R. Forty | F. Dalton Holmes | C. Pickering |
| A. D. Haller | C. Wells | C. F. Wells |
| H. E. Holmes | C. P. Wells | T. B. Holmes |
| R. P. Maw | H. D. Meek | Dr. Johns |
| M. Stirling | W. R. F. Collinson | E. Smith |
| H. D. Wells | Maj. B. Haworth Booth | H. J. Grummett |
| S. Harris | R. F. Jamieson | |

Other persons in the area considered suitable for membership were circulated and caddies were recruited at fees of 4 pence per round if they were 1st class caddies or 3 pence if 2nd class.

By the time the course was opened on Monday 1st August, Stanley Villa, Newbegin had been acquired on a five-year lease as a club house. W. Dell, a young man who had caddied at Ilkley for 6 years had been appointed as professional and green keeper to be on probation for 4 months at a salary of 20/- per week, and a total of 65 members had by now joined the club.

The opening day saw a good crowd of officials and members together with their wives congregating at the club house in Newbegin. They were joined by the vicars of Hornsea and Rise and Dr. Smart from Beeford. The club house included a club room at the front and at the rear a dressing room with 17 lockers for gentlemen members. On the second floor was a dressing room for ladies. Accommodation in

*The first Committee.*

13

the clubhouse was also provided for the Professional and Caretaker.

It had been hoped that Captain Constable could have performed the opening ceremony but in the event he was ably replaced by County Councillor Mr. T. B. Holmes J.P. The Captain, Mr. Gregson introduced him "as a most honoured citizen and enthusiastic golfer".

Mr. Holmes spoke of the pleasures and science of golf. He was glad that the game had not descended to the level of horse racing and that Sunday playing would not be permitted.

He declared the clubhouse open to a hearty round of applause and Mr. Gregson then presented him with a driver on behalf of the club. Three hearty cheers ended the ceremony.

The reports tell that an adjournment was then made to the links where, to quote the report at the time, "The situation is ideal and in summer will be a perfect picture of rural scenery. Here a photograph of the assembly was taken. The scarlet coats of the golfers relieved the monotony and gave colour to the surroundings. Mr. T. Gregson opened the links with a grand drive which evoked much cheering. A game was then played between Dell (the Hornsea "pro") and Tom Vardon, with Mr. T. P. Cooke as referee".

The report concludes with the fact that Dell was rather overawed by the occasion and was beaten by Vardon who scored 38 to Dell's 44. It went on "At the conclusion our representative interviewed Tom Vardon who observed: 'It is a very good sporting course and has wonderfully improved since my last visit. The first three holes should be,' he added, 'reached with four shots; the next two holes with three'. The sixth hole is in a very pretty situation beyond a large tree, and according to Vardon should, 'with perfect golf, be manoeuvred with three; whilst the remaining holes will take four efforts. The whole course consists of nine holes and is therefore only half the length of the ordinary distance. Later in the afternoon the members competed together in a game for a special silver medal commemorative of the auspicious event and many favourable comments were passed on the character of the ground for golf and exercise!"

To join the new Hornsea Golf Club cost a gentleman an entrance fee of £2.2s.0d. and an annual subscription of £1.1s.0d. For ladies it was £1.10s.0d. and 10s.6d. and a family ticket could be had for an entrance fee of £5.5s.0d. and an annual subscription of £3.3s.0d. Visitors were charged 2/- per day or 7/6d per week in winter but

14

# Hornsea Golf Club.

## CADDIES.

1.—Caddies are paid 10d. for one round, and 6d. for a short round not exceeding 9 holes, which charge includes the cleaning of the Clubs.

2.—Caddies will go out in rotation. Members must engage Caddies through the Caddie Master, or in his absence through the Caretaker, who will give a Ticket which at the end of the round mnst be given to the Caddie. It is requested that no money whatever be given to Caddies.

3.—Members may engage Caddies for any time or day, by previously notifying the Caddie Master. The Caddie Master will on that day engage Caddies (who will be taken in rotation) for such members.

4.—If a member, having previously engaged a Caddie, does not (weather permitting) turn up within an hour, the engagement shall be cancelled, and the member shall pay the Caddie for a round.

5.—Members must not purchase balls from Caddies. Caddies selling balls are liable to instant dismissal.

6.—Players are also requested to see that their Caddies replace all divots and to report to the Caddie Master any Caddie who shall fail to do this, or for insubordination or incapacity.

OCTOBER, 1908.

15

from June to August the charges rose to 2/6d and 10/6d and 15/-per fortnight or £1.1s.0d. for a month.

Saturday was the main golfing day in the week and caddies were ballotted for by members who had sent their names in by the previous evening. Initially the course was closed on Sunday and even a few years later, when it was finally opened on the Sabbath, no caddies, refreshments, or lessons were available.

*Hornsea Golf Club's first clubhouse in Newbegin is the farthest right of the photograph with an eagle on the post.*

The main competition was for a monthly badge but in 1899 the Grummett/McKenzie cup was presented to be competed for by the leading eight players in the October medal. During his captain's year in 1903, F. S. Broderick presented the cup to be named after him and to be played for at Whitsuntide each year as a bogey competition, and it was in 1909 that Mr. Maw presented his Scratch Cup to the club with specific instructions on the competition he envisaged, carefully set out in an accompanying letter.

Some of the first inter-club matches were played against Beverley and Brough golf clubs.

Unfortunately the initial euphoria which had accompanied the opening of the club did not last and problems soon began. The

16

TELEGRAMS "MAWS, SOLICITORS, HULL."
TELEPHONE Nº 934.

MAW & REDMAN,
SOLICITORS
AND
COMMISSIONERS FOR OATHS.

OCEAN CHAMBERS,
LOWGATE,

HULL 29ᵗʰ April 190 7

*Dear William .*

*I have taken up my Cup to the Club House, & asked Wingate to hand it to you.*

*The Conditions are*

*Scratch play . Medal round — to be played 1ˢᵗ Saturday in May, unless that date interferes with the Good Challenge Cup, when earliest possible date after shall be taken — First 4 (or 8 if the Committee should at any time prefer), to play off on succeeding Saturdays by match play. In the event of ties; in medal play to play off during the week — say Tuesday — unless mutually arranged otherwise; in match play to play on till one or the other wins a hole. No Entrance fee.*

*Yours faithfully,
Dick Maw*

course was felt to be too short to be a good test of golf and, worse still, members began to resign in considerable numbers. Some of these resignations were as a direct result of some other Links being opened in Hull.

In 1900, in an effort to attract new members, the entrance fee was abolished and to partially offset this loss in revenue, the professional Dell's wages were halved to 10/- per week. Although he was about to get married Dell accepted this reduction, possibly because the club offered him not only free accommodation in the clubhouse but

17

the use of two rooms there, originally set aside for lady members, to let for profit. However in 1901 he resigned to be replaced by a Mr. Finch from the North Surrey Club whose wife became the stewardess. The following year saw the first full time groundsman appointed.

*Professional's accounts for week-ending 5th June 1905.*

The conditions of service for the groundsman and his wife were set out in a letter to applicants:

> 'The wages are 18/- per week with rooms in Club House which is close to the links and in good situation. Rent and rates are free. A further sum of £5 is given out of which the caretaker would be expected to keep a fire in the club-room during the winter months from dinner-time to dusk, and all day on Saturdays, and to supply oil for the lamp in the club-room. A share of the Xmas box fund is also given to the groundsman and caretaker, which should bring in a further £3-£4. The general hours of work are, as groundsman 6.30—4, Saturdays 6.30 till 10. There is no Sunday play and the club is closed on Sundays.'

It was eventually decided to lengthen the course and some land belonging to a Mr. Clarke between Eastgate and Cliff Lane, which is now the Ashcourt Estate, was rented. Still remaining a nine-hole

18

course, it was redesigned to lengthen all the holes. Now players had six holes on the original land and were then required to cross the narrow Eastgate lane to play another three.

Great problems were experienced with both sections of the course because the landowners persisted in allowing horses to graze and this caused havoc with the greens. It was only when the club offered a higher rent that the problem was resolved.

Problems experienced with unruly and insubordinate caddies resulted in a Caddie Master being appointed in 1904 to work from 4.30 pm to close of play on ordinary days and from 9 am to 12 noon and 1 pm to close on Saturdays. Players with caddies had precedence on the course. No three or fourballs were allowed on Saturdays except when a member wanted to play in a competition, had no partner and the professional was not available to mark his card!

By 1906 the club was seriously looking at alternatives to their nine-hole course and again the fields at Rowlston were suggested. Major Haworth Booth had been a keen founder member of the club and resided at Rowlston Hall. He suggested that some of his fields might be used as a course but the general opinion was that the ground was too heavy and a sub-committee was appointed to widen the search.

In 1907 an extraordinary general meeting was called to discuss the matter and it was decided after all to move to a new 120 acre site at Rowlston. The club was no doubt persuaded by some very generous terms offered by the golf loving Major plus the fact that the English Open champion, Alec (Sandy) Herd had looked over the proposed land, considered it suitable, and submitted a plan for the new course.

At 6000 yards the new eighteen-hole course would be one of the longest in the East Riding and the Major offered to lay it out at his own expense and build a bungalow style club house at a cost of £1,000. He would only charge 5% of the cost of the building and lease the whole to the club for an initial 21 years. He would charge a nominal £50 per year rent for the first two years and then take 25% of subscriptions and green fees in lieu of rent. He agreed to pay any rates on the course if the club would pay rates on the club house. He retained the rights to graze sheep on the course and claimed a permanent seat on the club's executive committee. A benefactor indeed and a grateful club elected him President.

The club house was constructed by J. Levitt, a local contractor but the national seedsmen Carters were given the task of preparing

*Members of Hornsea Golf Club circa 1914 with venerable 'Old John Hollis' and C. H. Loncaster the captain seated centre.*

the course which duly opened on 3rd October 1908. The Holmes Ramsden trophy was presented the following year to mark the opening of the new course.

Herd's plan was to be varied twice in following years after consultations with famous golf architects Dr. McKenzie of Leeds and James Braid respectively. They proposed some drastic alterations to the very flat greens and suggested extensive bunkering. In 1914 it was to have hosted the Yorkshire second division championship but the outbreak of war intervened.

Unfortunately the move of venue did nothing to ease increasing financial problems which were to plague the club for many years. The overdraft in 1909 was £280 and increasing yearly. Again the generosity of Major Haworth Booth came to the rescue when he offered to forgo the rent for a year if members would raise £100 between them to offset the overdraft. A total of £127.6s. was raised and the Major promised to repeat his gesture the following year if necessary. Fortunately it was not until 1917 that the exercise had to be repeated and the Major not only forwent his rent but personally donated £25 towards a total of £268.13s. raised on this occasion.

The club just managed to tick over during the first World War, the professional had joined the colours and the ladies' section appears to have gone into complete limbo.

The end of the War saw a rash of staffing problems. Mr. White the professional returned from military service but his wife who had remained as stewardess had been falling into disfavour as on one occasion when she was reported for being rude and failing to execute orders. When cautioned by the Secretary about this the good lady grudgingly apologised and promised such amendment 'as her nature would permit!' The Whites resigned in 1919 and Mr. and Mrs. Boyd from Ramsey were appointed. The same year the first house committee was formed. In 1821 a Mr. McLachlan was given a trial as professional but was not successful and Mr. and Mrs. Armitage were appointed as professional and stewardess respectively. They were dismissed within twelve months and were succeeded in 1922 by Mr. and Mrs. Dailey. Through all this staff upheaval Mr. Donkin who joined the green staff from Brough Golf Club in 1915 remained. He was to last for 40 years and become the mainstay of the green staff.

*Cartoon by E. R. N. Shaw*
*1920.*

The club's ever present financial predicament was gravely exacerbated by the sudden death of Major Howarth Booth in 1920 when it transpired that a large portion of the golf course land had only been held by him on leasehold until his death. The new owners immediately announced it was for sale and put the club in a serious dilemma. It could not function without the land but had no fund of money available. Three possibilities were considered. They could do nothing and hope the land would find no purchaser or, make a bid at the auction or, try to buy privately prior to the sale. With either of the last two options finance was a stumbling block.

Members were circulated and there was strong support to buy the whole of the course and buildings and to form a limited

22

NORBURY-SMITH & CO.

## YORKSHIRE, EAST RIDING

# ROLSTON ESTATE, HORNSEA,

NEAR HULL.

### 1577 ACRES

Of excellent FREEHOLD ARABLE and PASTURE LANDS.

### 40 LOTS

(except such as may be sold by Private Treaty) comprising

ROLSTON HALL, a Fine Old medium-sized Mansion,
with 37 Acres of PARK LANDS.

—— NINE FERTILE FARMS ——

A Well-built RESIDENCE, and nearly Two Acres SMALL
HOLDINGS.

COTTAGES, WATERWORKS, Parcels of ALLOTMENTS,
Accommodation and Building LANDS.

RIFLE RANGE.

To be Offered for SALE BY AUCTION, in Lots, by

# NORBURY=SMITH & CO.

AT THE

HULL INCORPORATED LAW SOCIETY, Lincoln's Inn
Buildings, Bowlalley Lane, HULL,

*On Thursday, October 7th,* 1920,

Commencing at TWO o'clock.

Particulars, Plans, and Conditions of Sale may be obtained from
the AUCTIONEERS, 5, George Street, Hanover Square, London,
W.1. Telephone: Gerrard, 7872. 7167

*The sale that nearly ended Hornsea Golf Club.*

23

company with share and debenture issues providing the finance. On 10th August 1921 Hornsea Golf Club Ltd. was incorporated with a capital of £2,000 split into £5 shares. This was increased to £3,000 in January 1922. A total of 700 Debentures at £5 each were also issued carrying interest of 6% per annum. Together these issues raised a total of £4,735 and an overdraft facility of £5,000 was arranged with the Midland Bank which enabled all the club's assets including the land freehold to be purchased at a total cost of £8,036.

The first board meeting held at the Alexandra Hotel was chaired by Mr. H. E. Kirbus the club captain and Mr. H. A. Learoyd was elected company chairman for the first twelve months. The other founder directors were: M. G. Nightingale, J. H. Tate, A. S. Haller, A. H. Tyacke, H. E. Holmes and C. H. Loncaster.

Mr. W. P. Murdoch was appointed club manager and secretary at a salary of £125 per annum and the first annual report of the company in April 1922 spoke of the hard struggle the company would have to meet its financial commitments. Already, although the great majority of 153 men and 79 lady members had taken up their shares, difficulty was experienced in getting the money from a few and the ultimate sanction of dismissal had to be imposed in some cases. For the next twenty or thirty years lack of money continued to be a problem for the club and it became a routine and well remembered exercise on Saturday afternoons in the men's smoke room for a collection to be made to help to pay the staff wages. Claude Lax who joined the club in 1927 remembers the ritual weekend gathering in the club house after golf, when drinks would be obtained from stewardess Mrs. Hammond at the bar and all would retire to the smoke room (the men's old card room) for a drink and chat. Mrs. Hammond would visit the room to take further orders and one day young Lax was surprised to find his father pushing a ten shilling note into his hand. The reason soon became obvious when Tommy Wells appeared with his cap. Lax senior put £1 in and Claude's ten shillings followed.

Tommy Wells, local auctioneer, Peter Ramsden, manager of the Hornsea branch of the Midland Bank and P. R. Davis or PRD as he was known, were a formidable triumvirate of power at the club during the inter-war years.

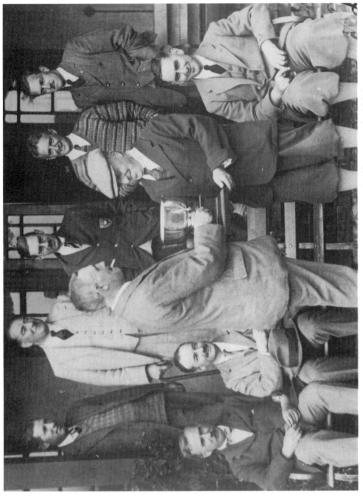

*Presentation by Captain J. H. Tate to A. E. Havercroft 1924.*
*Left to right: ?, P. R. Davies, Norman Allen, Arthur Pratt, Geoffrey Shackles, Mr. Tate,*
*A. E. Havercroft, Peter Ramsden, Clive Sutton, Percy Hornby.*

25

Early years saw Hornsea Public Rooms hired for the annual golf club ball. A piano together with special floor polish was always ordered from Hull for the event, the former being hired for the day. Transport being difficult it became a regular feature for the club to hire a complete special train to run from Hull to Hornsea at the start of the evening, stopping at all stations and returning after the ball. Individual dance programmes were printed as well as impressive tickets and menu cards.

As years went by some events were able to be held in the Rolston Road club house but major dinners and dances are still to this day taken away from the club. Despite the club's general financial problems an active social life was always present and dances, dinners, bridge and whist drives have always been popular and well attended throughout the 100 years.

The outbreak of War in 1939 saw immediate economies made. The two waitresses were dismissed, two green staff were paid off, the course was let for sheep grazing at 4 pence per animal per week. It was agreed members called up for service would be honorary members for the duration.

Camp beds were put in the upstairs room of the club house to enable members travelling from Hull and elsewhere to stay overnight at weekends. They would catch the midday train from Hull to Hornsea Bridge where a taxi met them by arrangement and took them to the course and it would collect them in time to catch the late afternoon train back on Sunday afternoon. The club captain in 1940 (F. W. Harrison) was forced to resign after only a few months because he was posted elsewhere on military duties. More green staff were sacked in 1940 and the salaries of the secretary and Treasurer were reduced. Members of Hornsea Home Guard were made non-playing members of the club for the duration. In 1941 Donkin and Taylor the two remaining green staff were paid overtime to do haymaking on the course.

The War forced the club to ask debenture holders to forgo interest for the duration. In addition an appeal was made to members for loans to allow the club to carry on. A total of £337 was raised by this method and many of the lenders made their loans into gifts when war ended. Somehow this money was eked out to cover expenses until 1945. Unfortunately the post war years did nothing to relieve the financial burden of running the golf club and it was not until well into the 1980s that the problem of money

Mementos of Club Social Events.

A. 907

Mrs Stanley Earle
Hornsea

PARCELS DEPARTMENT,
Hornsea STATION, &c

Dear 8 - 190//

To the NORTH EASTERN RAILWAY COMPANY, Dr.

Cheques in discharge of Accounts to be made payable to the Order of the North Eastern Railway Company.
The Directors require carriage and other charges to be paid on delivery of Merchandise unless an account has been opened with the Company.
Packages weighing 336 lbs. and under will be charged in accordance with the Small Parcels Scale.

Dec 2nd   Cost of Special Train, Hornsea
          to Hull   Dec 2nd 1911          £1/1/0

          Paid Dec 11th 1911
          E Pickup

23

HORNSEA GOLF CLUB.
(LADIES' SECTION).

A BRIDGE DRIVE

WILL BE HELD AT THE ABOVE CLUB

On MONDAY, OCTOBER 28th, 1929,

AT 2-30 P.M.

Tickets 2/6 each.

27

## Hornsea Golf Club.

### Fourth Annual Dance

Public Rooms, Hornsea.

Friday, the 5th December, 1913.

M.C.'s:

Mr. R. REYNOLDS.
Mr. R. P. MAW.

Stewards:

| | |
|---|---|
| Col. A. L. FLODMAN. | Mr. H. E. KIRRUS. |
| Major J. R. HEDLEY. | Mr. W. COBBY. |
| Mr. J. H. TATE. | Mr. R. M. ALEXANDER. |
| Mr. TOM WELLS. | |

RICHD. JOHNSON AND BONS HULL

### Programme

| Dances. | Engagements. |
|---|---|
| 1. Valse — *The Girl on the Film* | 1 |
| 2. Valse — *Laughing Husband* | 2 |
| 3. Two-Step — *On the Mississippi* | 3 |
| 4. Valse — *Marriage Market* | 4 |
| 5. Lancers — *Sunshine Girl* | 5 |
| 6. Valse — *Oh! Oh! Delphine* | 6 |
| 7. One-Step — *Puppchen* | 7 |
| 8. Valse — *Nights of Gladness* | 8 |
| 9. Valse — *Dancing Mistress* | 9 |

| | |
|---|---|
| 1. EXTRA | 2. EXTRA |
| 3. EXTRA | 4. EXTRA |

| Dances. | Engagements. |
|---|---|
| 10. Two-Step — *Wedding Glide* | 10 |
| 11. Valse — *Un Peu d'Amour* | 11 |
| 12. Valse — *Dreaming* | 12 |
| 13. Lancers — *Gipsy Love* | 13 |
| 14. Valse — *Little grey home in the West* | 14 |
| 15. One-Step — *You made me love you* | 15 |
| 16. Valse — *The Spring Maid* | 16 |
| 17. Valse — *A Thousand Kisses* | 17 |

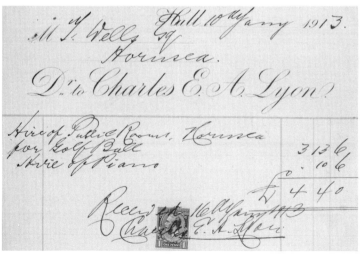

Hull 10th Jan'y 1913.

Mr. T. Wells Esq
Hornsea.

Dr. to Charles E. A. Lyon.

Hire of Public Rooms, Hornsea
for Golf Ball — 3 13 6
Hire of Piano — 0 . 10 6

£ 4 4 0

Received 16th Jan'y 1913
Charles E. A. Lyon

ONE PENNY

28

29

ceased to be an overwhelming worry.

In the early 1950s the club was so desperate for money that sweepstakes were held and members were again asked for loans, some of which were rewarded with life membership. The club's bank in Hornsea was constantly worrying about the overdraft and eventually the account was changed to another bank. The officials here seemed much more sympathetic to the problems particularly when the Branch Manager joined the club and became an enthusiastic member.

This period also saw the sale of the strip of land bordering Rolston Road from the club house to the main practice green. Plots were offered first to members and then to the general public at £200-£300 each.

Over the years the club arranged for a number of nationally well known professional golfers to visit and give exhibitions.

*Hornsea team plus officials who tied with Kirkella Golf Club in the Hull & District Competition 1951.*

The first of which there is a record was in 1914, just before the start of the Great War when The Imperial Hydro Hotel, Hornsea, sponsored a match between Harry Vardon and George Duncan. Duncan was to return later in 1923 to play an exhibition match against the American, Abe Mitchell, when each player was rewarded with 12 guineas plus expenses.

In the 1930s P. R. Davies was always keen to promote both club and course. He was also a very great fan of Henry Cotton, then in his

31

*Henry Cotton plays at Hornsea Golf Club.*

prime. Davies asked the club's new professional Stan Stenhouse to try and arrange for Cotton to visit Hornsea and on 7th May 1931, arguably the most famous golfing visitor to the Club arrived in the person of Henry Cotton. He came with Archie Cromston and a large crowd watched as the two famous professionals were taken on by Stenhouse and Bill Stout from Bridlington. The local men won the match but it has to be said that Cotton himself was not at all well, suffering as he was from a stomach ulcer. During the day his glamorous wife 'Toots' caused some outrage among members when she stalked across the hallowed putting green in her high heeled shoes.

Walter Hagan visited and played in Hornsea in 1933.

In 1938 Stan Stenhouse was playing in the British Open, held at the Carnoustie course for the first time. The full American Ryder Cup team had entered prior to playing in the Cup itself. Again at the instigation of P. R. Davies, when Stenhouse got to Carnoustie he approached the manager of the American team and asked if two of their players could visit Hornsea. This was agreed and on the Sunday after the Ryder Cup finished Ed. Dudley and Horton Smith arrived at Hornsea and played against Stan Stenhouse and Ed. Fallon.

Probably the best remembered visit was on 8th May 1966 when Sam Sharp arranged for Peter Allis, Dai Rees, Bernard Hunt and Dave Thomas to come to the club to play a fourball exhibition.

*Alan Hardaker of the Football League.*
*Guest of Honour at the Club Dinner 1974.*

Other well known players to visit Hornsea included Sunsmore and Shuter.

By the time the club had moved into its ninetieth year the climate for golf had undergone a transformation. Television had persuaded the population at large that the game was worth watching and playing. More and more applications were received for membership and waiting lists were instituted. Subscription income increased and there was an enormous growth in the number of visiting parties, and 'fruit' machines had arrived to help boost club income. Hornsea exploited the change in fortunes by investing much of the income back into the club. The course and facilities were enhanced. A new Professional shop, new Halfway House, new equipment sheds, new watering systems and a complete refurbishment of the club house have all put the club in excellent heart to face the next 100 years.

## Chapter 2
## The Course at Rolston

The part of Major Howarth-Booth's land selected to be the course at Rowlston or Rolston provided plenty of room to plan a challenging golf layout. Natural features were however few and far between on what was basically a flat treeless area. The clay soil, while retaining moisture well, meant the Hornsea greens would never quite compare with courses such as Ganton because of an inability to produce the finest type of grasses.

*The original Club House.*

Until the middle of the nineteenth century a large part of the land to be used for the new golf course would have been part of the middle field of Rowlston village. It would have been farmed by villagers in the traditional strip fashion and tilled by the ridge and furrow method so leaving the series of ridges so familiar to those playing many of the fairways at Hornsea Golf Club today.

Initial laying out of the course was carried out by Alex (Sandy)

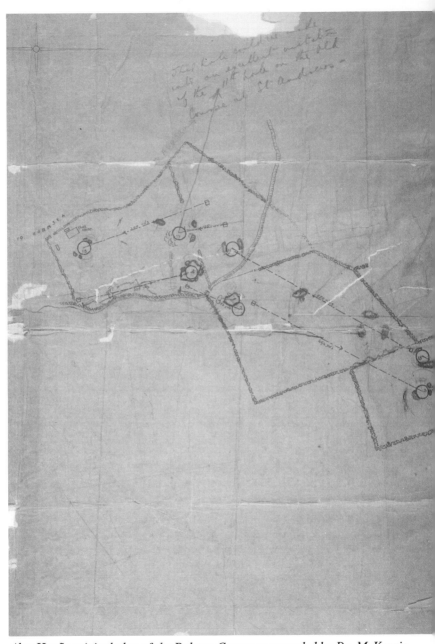

*Alex Herd's original plan of the Rolston Course as amended by Dr. McKenzie.*

36

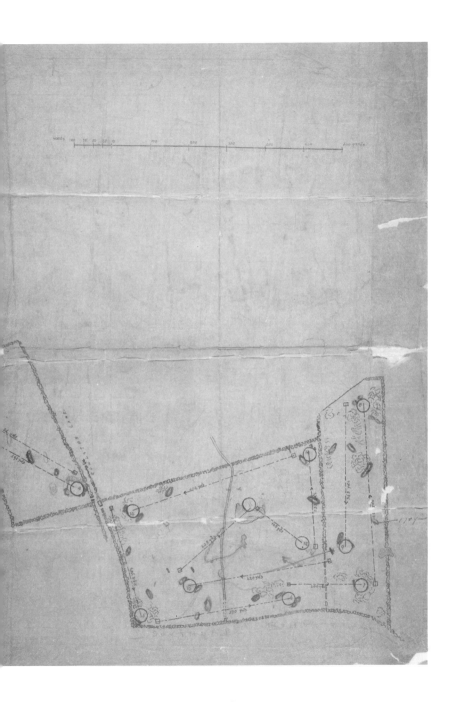

Herd the then English golf champion. With a length of 5927 yards it was one of the longest in the East Riding. Some major differences existed compared to the course in 1998 and Mr. Herd's hand drawn proposals can still be seen today, carefully amended in pencil by succeeding architects employed.

The holes were as follows:

| 1. | 300 yds. | Par 4 | 10. | 420 yds. | Par 5 |
|---|---|---|---|---|---|
| 2. | 156 yds. | 3 | 11. | 235 yds. | 4 |
| 3. | 494 yds. | 6 | 12. | 165 yds. | 3 |
| 4. | 391 yds. | 5 | 13. | 237 yds. | 4 |
| 5. | 294 yds. | 4 | 14. | 442 yds. | 5 |
| 6. | 370 yds. | 5 | 15. | 430 yds. | 5 |
| 7. | 200 yds. | 4 | 16. | 556 yds. | 6 |
| 8. | 471 yds. | 5 | 17. | 120 yds. | 3 |
| 9. | 362 yds. | 5 | 18. | 300 yds. | 4 |
|  | 3028 yds. | 41 |  | 2899 yds. | 39 |

The main most noticeable differences with today's course would be firstly the second hole. Here the tee what is now the current men's winter tee but the green was just at the top of the bank, a par three, reached by climbing a stile in the valley.

*Playing out of the bunker. Guarding the second hole.*
Photo by Turner and Drinkwater, Regent House, Hull.

*Putting on the sixth green.*
Photo by Turner & Drinkwater, Regent House, Hull.

*Driving from the twelfth teeing ground,*
*showing approach across the pond at the eleventh hole on to the green,*
*behind, the caddy in the foreground.*
Photo by Turner & Drinkwater, Regent House, Hull.

The tee for hole three was also at the top of the bank with the hole being completely straight to the present third green. No dog leg!

The sixth hole was much shorter than today, the twelfth tee to the basin hole was behind the pond and the thirteenth tee was the current men's winter tee with a straight 237 yard shot to the old green.

The sixteenth was a massive 556 yards from the current yellow tee to a green in the centre of the present practice ground and to the west of the present seventeenth green.

The seventeenth tee was the present ladies' eighteenth and the green was in the middle of the gorse and trees at the top of what is today the Professional's practice ground. Dr. MacKenzie was later reported as saying it would have made a marvellous copy of the famous 11th on the Old Course at St. Andrews.

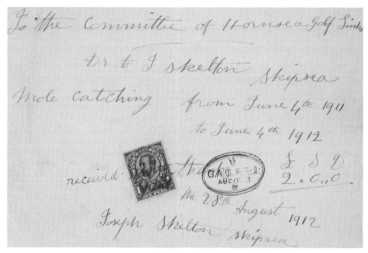

In fact, four years after opening the Rolston course the advice of Dr. MacKenzie who lived at Leeds, was sought. Dr. Alistair Mac-Kenzie, a former G.P. at both Normanton and Leeds had taken to the profession of golf architecture and regularly placed advertisements of his skills in the magazine *Golfing*. In his later years he listed over 50 courses in which he had been involved including Ganton and Hornsea. Eventually he emigrated to America where he was responsible for among others, Cypress Point and the famous Augusta courses. He died before seeing the first shot played at the latter.

When he came to Hornsea he considered in general the course was very good but made a number of recommendations, particularly in relation to the greens. He himself was convinced all greens should be visible to approaching players and have an undulating surface rising towards the back (MacKenzie greens). He considered all the Hornsea greens except the sixth were too flat. Some but not all of his ideas were implemented by the club.

# GREEN FEES

should be paid BEFORE play is commenced and Tickets retained for production on the Course, if requested.

**Press Bell on Right for Ticket.**

As a result of MacKenzie's recommendations the card for the course was altered as follows:

| | | | | | | |
|---|---|---|---|---|---|---|
| 1. | 300 yds. | Par 4 | 10. | 410 yds. | Par 5 |
| 2. | 160 yds. | 3 | 11. | 237 yds. | 4 |
| 3. | 516 yds. | 6 | 12. | 167 yds. | 3 |
| 4. | 391 yds. | 5 | 13. | 235 yds. | 4 |
| 5. | 298 yds. | 4 | 14. | 444 yds. | 5 |
| 6. | 379 yds. | 5 | 15. | 434 yds. | 6 |
| 7. | 200 yds. | 4 | 16. | 440 yds. | 5 |
| 8. | 464 yds. | 5 | 17. | 130 yds. | 3 |
| 9. | 364 yds. | 5 | 18. | 390 yds. | 5 |
| | | **41** | | | **40** |

In August 1924 James Braid, professional golfer, winner of five Open Championships and a course architect with clubs such as Carnoustie, Gleneagles and Dalmahoy under his belt, was asked to

*The pond hole circa 1940, with thatched shelter which blew away in gales.*
*The bare nature of the course compared to 1998 can be clearly seen.*

again review the course. He made a number of recommendations particularly relating to bunkering, some of the more interesting being as follows:

(a) Take the sixth green back over the ridge at the back which made it the present two-tier green.
(b) Move the seventh tee nearer to the gate.
(c) Move the ninth green further back on to the higher ground so that it could be seen by approaching golfers at an earlier stage.

November 1908 had seen the purchase of the first horse for the club to pull mowers and rollers on the fairways. The days of motorised mowing machines were in the offing and although the club purchased its first old tractor in 1926, horses were retained until 1939. At one committee meeting on 10th March 1921 Mr. J. H. Tate solemnly proposed and Mr. Ramsden seconded a motion that 'Old Jack be shot'. It is assumed Old Jack must have been the horse!

*Punting on the Pond between the Wars.*

Horses finally became redundant when member Don Noble purchased a small Ford tractor for £150 and presented it to the club.

In the early days much of the grass was kept reasonably short by Major Howarth-Booth's sheep and the greens required fencing against the animals.

Through all the trials and tribulations and hard work connected with developing the new course, Greensman Donkin, long serving and loyal servant of the club, never failed in his efforts to care for the Rolston Course.

The 1914-18 War saw both club and course slip into a state of suspended animation. The 1939-45 War also saw many economies and the condition of the course deteriorated. Greens were cut much smaller and outer areas were lost for the duration. Part of the course was ploughed up for corn and by 1943, because of the amount of grass growing in the bunkers, clubs were allowed to be grounded. 1946 saw the club accepting the loan of an American Jeep to help in restoring the course and six Italian prisoners-of-war were engaged on similar work.

Water supplies had always been a problem and in 1908 a well had been sunk which was it was claimed could supply some 600 gallons per day but it was very poor quality water. Water for the greens had to be taken by bucket and in 1924 consideration was given to installing a pump. The arrival of Hull water in Hornsea made the

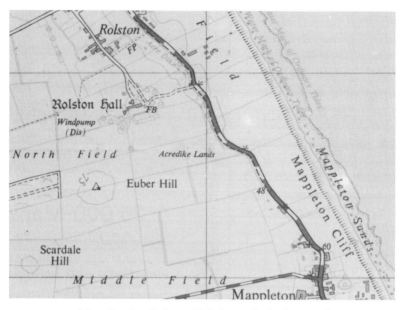

*Map showing Rolston Hall formerly the home of
Major Haworth Booth and Euber Hill.*

old town water works at Euber Hull redundant. Euber Hull being conveniently situated just to the south east of the 8th green consideration was given to utilising it for the club. Sometime during 1936 or 1937 someone, believed to be either P. R. Davies or Tim Tomlinson, decided to purchase the works on behalf of the club without any consultation with other officials. The club eventually accepted the *fait accompli* and water was laid from the works to some, but not all, the greens. It was not an ideal situation and the pumps kept breaking down. Eventually the decision was taken to tap into the main Hull supply by the sixth fairway and water was then piped to all the greens.

The operation cost £1,000 and in 1964 the now derelict Ebor or Euber Hill works were sold.

*Euber or Ebor Hill Waterworks.*

Money still being short in the 1950s the club decided to sell a strip of land by the side of the eighteenth fairway and fronting Rolston Road for housing development. Members were given first chance to buy the plots which were priced between £200-£300 each.

Drainage was always a problem on the course and many efforts to drain fairways were made over the years and particularly in the 1970s when extensive work was carried out. The hard work and money spent on drainage has now had a dramatically beneficial effect on the course in winters.

Landscaping the course with trees began in earnest after the second World War ended. Over 750 ash and leylandi trees were planted as a first phase and the programme continued and indeed increased over the years to the present day which has completely changed the appearance and character of the area.

Because of the increasing cost of water together with a number of years of low rainfall, it was decided to construct a large lake/-reservoir holding 15 million gallons of water, between the 10th and 14th holes in 1990. In 1991 an automatic sprinkler system was installed throughout the course. The year 1996 was the first to fully test the new arrangements with little rainfall during summer and autumn. The lake was used constantly and the level dropped

*Digging the Reservoir in 1990.*

*Old and new 13th green October 1993.*
*With new green under construction far right of photograph.*

dramatically but, when the rains returned it had survived and served its purpose and soon refilled.

In 1991 a venerable and well loved halfway house was considered inadequate and replaced by a splendid new version.

Hornsea Golf Club have been fortunate in the quality of many long serving ground staff and Roger Bielby has been an outstanding first full time manager of the course since 1978.

*Roger Bielby.*

Roger, a member of a well known local family, started farming on leaving school. He and his brothers were encouraged to become golfers by their late father and one went on to join the professional ranks.

Persuaded by Mike Hesk, then chairman of the Greens to take up golf course work, Roger joined the Green staff in 1977. Since his arrival the course has developed into one of the finest in the area.

Not only an expert Greenkeeper, Roger is a fine golfer. He has represented the East Riding Golf Union on over 100 occasions and has served as President of that body.

47

## Chapter 3
## Snippets from "The Snug"

Most, if not all golf clubs have been blessed with a room where male members would gather to discuss both women-folk and trivial matters relating to the club, the town, the country and indeed the world. Hornsea had its 'Snug Bar' for this important function and it seemed therefore an appropriate title for a section of the book devoted to odd pieces of information which have come to notice during its compilation.

Progress has meant that the old 'snug' bar, scene of many a passionate debate, was radically altered in 1997 into a spike bar, games room and card room combined. The cosy atmosphere of this previously men only cubbyhole was first shattered in the early 1990s when its sanctity was breached by the arrival of a few lady members who demanded and were allowed access. It saw the end of the mens' traditional snug, and it is hoped this part of the centenary book will form a suitable memorial to a much loved albeit rather grubby, room.

What follows are a collection of odd, interesting and sometimes amusing extracts from club and newspaper records together with recollections of some of the older members.

At the club's inception club dress and colours were adopted as a scarlet jacket with green collar and cuffs and monogrammed buttons.

In 1905 the custom of sending drinks out to members on the course was stopped.

In April 1906 the GPO announced they were willing to bring the telephone to Hornsea providing they could get a minimum of twenty subscribers at £7.15 per annum plus 3d. a call. They had obtained nineteen subscribers but could get no more and so the golf club decided to become the twentieth and were thus instrumental in bringing the telephone to the town as Hornsea 20, figures which remain in the club telephone number to this day!

The 11th-12th June 1909 saw the first open meeting held at Hornsea Golf Club.

Suggestion books exist from the earliest days of the club in which members could bring their views to the attention of those in authority and a number of the early entries are of interest. One gentleman suggested the North Eastern Railway be approached to recognise Hornsea as a golf club for which 'Golf Tickets' could be issued. Another rather more irate member suggested that the club committee 'confine themselves to matters of golf and leave members to watch over their own moral and religious affairs!'

Sunday play was allowed at Hornsea Golf Club for the first time when they moved to the new course at Rolston but no caddies or refreshments were available on this day. Even so many local people objected strongly to games on the Sabbath and an 830 signature petition was raised against the golf club by the Reverend A. T. Reissmann of Grosvenor Lodge. Among the points made in the petition was the following. "We cannot but regard Sunday golf as an encouragement for others who cannot afford its pleasures to indulge in other kinds of amusements like Football and Cricket on Sundays".

The 1914-18 War saw part of the club house dining room rented to the military with just three tables reserved for members.

Rangers were appointed by the club in 1923 to observe and report members who did not replace divots!

Land was sold above the 6th green in 1926 to Hull Water Co. for them to build a water tower. A total of 3866 square yards were sold for £150.

The year 1930 saw electricity brought to the club house and the Yorkshire Union 2nd division open was held at Hornsea. A marquee was obtained from Hull Brewery for the event but despite this and the electric light, the union said no more such competitions could be held at Hornsea until the club house accommodation had been improved.

Unfortunately 1931 saw entrance fees abolished in a desperate effort to attract new members and the following year saw the club in such dire financial straits that work on draining fairways had to stop for lack of money.

One week-end cigarettes ran out and the Secretary, Jack Fletcher apologised to members saying that if he had ordered more supplies the club cheque would have 'bounced'.

Tom Thirsk, member at Bridlington and Ganton was made an honorary member of Hornsea in recognition of his success in winning the golf competition at the 1936 (Hitler's) Olympic Games

# SUNDAY GOLF PETITION.

To the Members of the Hornsea Golf Club.

We, the undersigned residents of Hornsea, being over 16 years of age, have heard with intense sorrow that the New Golf Links are to be opened for play on Sundays, and would respectfully and earnestly appeal to the members of the Club to re-consider the whole question of Sunday Golf before it is too late.

We urge this for the following reasons:—

1. Many of us have come to reside in the town because of the rest and quietness which is enjoyed here on the Sabbath Day.

2. We cannot but feel that Sunday Golf will draw a large number of people to the town, especially during the summer months, who have no respect whatever for the quietness and sanctity of the Sabbath.

3. We have heard that very few of the members of the Club who reside in the town intend Golfing on Sundays, and fail to see why the quietness of the town should be disturbed for the pleasure of those who do not live here.

4. We are aware that at present no caddies are to be employed nor refreshments served, but once Sunday Golf is started in earnest the demand both for caddies and refreshments will increase and will have to be met, and we deprecate anything of the nature of increased facilities in this direction which necessarily will involve additional Sunday labour.

5. We moreover feel strongly that the influence of Sunday Golf upon the young life of our town will be most detrimental.

6. We cannot but regard Sunday Golf as an encouragement for others who cannot afford its pleasures to indulge in other kinds of amusements, such as Football and Cricket on the Sunday.

7. Although the links are outside the town, visitors who come over for the Sunday to play will be seen in our streets carrying their clubs, and in addition, the very knowledge that Sunday Golf is played locally will create an atmosphere which will be the greatest hindrance to all moral and religious work in our midst, especially amongst the young.

8. In a word, we believe that Sunday Golf will be disastrous to the best interests of the town.

We therefore urge the Club very earnestly to re-consider the question of Sunday Golf and to preserve the quietness and guard the sanctity of the Sabbath Day which we have so long enjoyed.

S. Haller, Westholme, Hornsea.

L. Grassby Westholme Hornsea

M. J. Buttimer

Maria Barnes, Hornsea.

Chas. B. Beresford, Hornsea

E. E. Parker 12 Cliff Terrace Hornsea

A. S. Parker  "  "  "

J. Coulson . Hornsea

S. A. Coulson  "

R. T. Buttimer Cliff Villas Hornsea

W. Snowdon jun 1 Clifton Terrace Hornsea

L. Snowdon              do              do

R. Snowdon              do              do

J. Snowdon              do              do

K. Snowdon              "              "

L. Snowdon              "              "

C. C. Hart          3   -do-          -do-

A. G. Anderton  the Gowans Cliff Road Hornsea

Margaret Anderton The Gowans

50

in Germany and for his excellent play generally in international golf. The same year saw the eminent Hull businessman Sir Alfred Gelder become a member.

Two holes were named after prominent early members in 1938 — the fourth was christened "Wells" and the eleventh "Haworth Booth". When and how they got changed again to their present names is not known.

In 1941, at the height of the Second World War, RAF Catfoss served a Requisition Order on the entire club house which was only withdrawn after the most strenuous representations.

Times were still hard in 1947 and the club decided that since it could not afford to continue presenting spoons or tankards as replicas for club cups, members were to be asked to return any old spoons which they had so that they could be re-used.

The smoke room fireplace was built of brick and members were encouraged to buy a brick for 2s.6d. to raise money for the club.

Between the wars it was quite easy to complete the 18 holes in 2 hours 30 minutes because so few were playing. Beth Smith recalls playing on summer Sundays, taking a picnic tea to eat by the gorse bushes on the 8th and having a leisurely half hour in the punt on the pond hole looking for balls. It was unlikely anyone would have asked to 'come through'.

In 1951 the golf club kitchen garden was sold to the club professional T. G. Bielby, at 2/6d per quare yard for him to build himself a house. This became known subsequently as the Pro's House.

In August 1967, because of the strong feelings of the club professional, Percy Wright, that he could not successfully combine the position with that of head greenkeeper, the latter post was advertised. There were only three applicants including Roger Bielby but the matter was not taken any further because of the club's inability to fund the post.

When Tim Tomlinson retired as chairman of the club in 1968, he presented the Tomlinson Family Cup to the club.

On 5th May 1969 despite protest from Jack Major that he had not suggested such a course, his company Hird Major & Co., Accountants, took over the club's secretarial duties for a six months trial period. The fee was to be between £300-£400. An assistant Secretary was to be appointed at a fee of £150 p.a. to look after day to day running.

On 24th June 1969 J. L. Major was appointed Secretary/-Treasurer of the club and Mrs. J. L. Major became minutes secretary.

In the late 1980s the club dining room was refurbished and the old wallpaper stripped. To everyone's surprise the walls revealed were covered with exotic and cleverly painted murals depicting the interior of a classical Grecian style restaurant complete with three-piece orchestra. The work of art is now reconcealed behind the present wall covering.

## Chapter 4
## From the Ladies' Lounge

Although Hornsea Golf Club was formed by men, ladies were accepted as members from the start. Not being very well organised in the early days however, the Section almost died away during the 1914-18 War, so much so that the men invited some ladies to tea in 1919 in order that they could elect officers and recommence playing.

Fairly severe restrictions were placed on the first lady members. In 1922 they were grudgingly allowed to tee off between 1 pm and 3 pm on a Saturday, **providing no men were waiting!** A year later attempts to remove restrictions on ladies playing on bank holidays were rejected and the hard won Saturday concession was unanimously withdrawn by the Board in 1926.

It was in that year that a young Mary Kirkus (née Davies) joined the club as a junior member. When she sadly passed away in 1994 she had been a member continuously for 68 years.

POINTS OF INTEREST:

In November 1907 the *Hull Daily Mail* reported that "the bowl presented by the president — Mrs. Haworth Booth, was won by Mrs. Inge Flodman with an excellent round of 54 out and 52 in = 106".

The year 1912 saw the newly opened Rolston Road course hosting the East Riding Ladies Amalgamated meeting at which the first and second prizes were presented by Mrs. Learoyd. First prize was a silver and tortoiseshell inlaid box value £2 and second, a silver fox valued at £1.1s.0d. The lady members of Hornsea presented a special prize of a silver watch valued at £1.10s.0d.

53

*President*—Major B. HAWORTH-BOOTH, J.P.
*Captain*—R. P. MAW, Esq.
*Hon. Secretary*—W. RUTTER SMITH, Esq.
*Hon. Treasurer*—L. LIVERSIDGE, Esq.
*Lady President*—Mrs HAWORTH-BOOTH, Rolston Hall, Hornsea.
*Ladies' Captain*—Mrs F. S. BRODRICK, Eastgate, Hornsea
*Ladies' Hon. Secretary*—Mrs C. F. WELLS, Suffolk Terr., Hornsea
*Ladies' Committee*—Mrs F. S. BRODRICK, Mrs B. C. BOLTON, Miss I. FLODMAN, Mrs LEAROYD, Mrs R. P. MAW, Mrs C. F. WELLS.

This Club has adopted L.G.U. Handicaps.

| L.G.U. and Hcp. | *List of Members* |
|---|---|
| 18 | Miss Alexander, Pembrook Villas, Hornsea |
| 13 | Miss F. Beaumont, Bank Terrace, Hornsea |
| 20 | Mrs Beresford, The Cottage, Cliff Lane |
| 19 | Mrs Bolton, Suffolk Terrace, Hornsea |
| 27 | Mrs Brodrick, Eastgate |
| 13 | Mrs Earle, Burton Road, Hornsea |
| 9 | Miss I. Flodman, Eastgate, Hornsea |
| 16 | Miss Flodman, Eastgate, Hornsea |
| 23 | Mrs Hobson, Lauriston, Ferriby Road, Hessle |
| 18 | Mrs A. S. Holmes, Analaby Road, Hull |
| 26 | Mrs Learoyd, Newbegin, Hornsea |
| 9 | Mrs R. P. Maw, Towers Close, Hornsea |
| 30 | Miss Milestone, "Southfield," Hornsea |
| 19 | Mrs Reynolds, Brampton House, Hornsea |
| 29 | Mrs Todd, Victoria Avenue, Hornsea |
| 21 | Mrs Watson |
| 10 | Miss S. Wells, 2 Suffolk Terrace, Hornsea |
| 22 | Mrs C. F. Wells, 2 Suffolk Terrace, Hornsea |

Miss E. Beaumont, Miss Bethell, Mrs Gaydon, Miss Cobby, Miss Dyson, Mrs J. W. Dossor, Mrs Good, Miss Grummitt, Mrs Grummitt, Miss Hart, Mrs Howarth-Booth, Miss Kemp, Miss White, Miss Sutton, Mrs Rutter-Smith, Mrs Marshall Ringrose, Miss Todd, Mrs Percy Wells

PRIZE WINNERS, 1907.
May 20th, Captain's Prize (R. P. Maw), Mrs Earle.
June 22nd, Prizes given by Mrs C. F. Wells,—Swatfest Tournament—First, Mrs Alexander ; second, Mrs Beresford.
June Challenge Cup, Mrs Earle, match play.
June 30th, Ladies Captain's Prize (Mrs R. P. Maw), Miss I. Flodman.
September 26th, Prizes presented by Mrs Butter Smith (mixed Foursomes), tie between Mr and Mrs Learoyd and Mr A. Cobby and Miss Alexander.
October 3rd, Prize presented by Mrs C. F. Wells, Miss M. Todd, 114—30=84.
October 24th, Lady President's Bowl (scratch), Miss I. Flodman, 106 gross.
December 26th, Prize presented by Mrs C. F. Wells (mixed Foursomes), Miss S. Wells and Mr H. E. Holmes, 97—7½=89½.
L.G.U. Silver Medal for Four Best Scores during year, Mrs S. Earle.

In 1921 the new board of directors received a complaint from the ladies section concerning the state of the female lavatories. The Board rather ungallantly replied that in their view "it was only necessary to encourage the ladies to use more earth!!"

April 1st the same year saw the Directors giving permission for a magazine to be ordered for the Ladies' lounge and after much discussion it was agreed this should be *The Gentlewoman*. The matter would be reviewed after a trial period.

July 1925 saw the presentation by Mr. R. S. Gray of a 'Cottage Hospital' Cup to be played for by the ladies.

September 25th the same year saw the Scratch Howarth Booth Cup being won by Mrs. Holmes with a score of 95. Second was Miss S. Wakeley with 102.

The Board would not agree to a suggestion from the ladies in 1927 that one hard and two grass tennis courts should be provided at the club.

In 1928 the ladies organised a dance the profits of which provided a cup to be played for at their open meeting.

The Yorkshire Ladies Challenge Bowl was held at Hornsea in June 1928, the first occasion a county ladies event had been held at the club.

The present ladies' lounge and changing rooms were added to the club house in 1932.

August 1934 saw Mrs. Stanley Earle become Ladies' Secretary, a post she was to hold for the next 25 years.

Later the same year, in November, the club presented commem-

*Yorkshire Challenge Bowl meeting in 1928 at Hornsea Golf Club.*
*The formidable lady in the centre is thought to be Mrs. Howarth Booth the Hornsea Ladies' President.*

*Yorkshire Interclub Championship 1934 – Hornsea.*
*Back left to right: Miss Cuttill, Miss Davis; Centre: Mrs. Todd, Mrs. Frost,*
*Mrs. Johnson (Capt.), Mrs. Barr; Front: Miss Johnson, Mrs. Proctor.*

-orative brooches to the members of the team who won the Yorkshire inter-club championship.

A restriction on ladies teeing off before 11 am on Sunday was introduced by the club in 1936.

The outbreak of War in 1939 saw the women buckling to and making new curtains for the club house.

In August 1959 Mrs. Stanley Earle retired after her marathon period in the post of Ladies' Secretary.

In 1968 the club celebrated its Diamond Jubilee. As part of the celebrations a four-ball better ball competition was arranged and it was agreed both men and women could compete. To the absolute astonishment of all the men two ladies won. This was so unexpected no prizes suitable for ladies had been obtained and the winners were presented with gentlemen's travelling razors which had to be exchanged later.

*L. G. U. Silver Division Challenge Bowl meeting.*
*Hornsea June 10th, 1936.*

### Outstanding Achievements by Ladies

No record of the Hornsea Ladies Section would be complete without mentioning some of the great achievements by both individuals and teams during the last 100 years.

Arguably the best lady golfer to play from Hornsea was Mary Johnson from 'Westfield' Cliff Road, in the town. A home grown member, daughter of a well known local family who were tailors in Hull famous for their displays of naval uniforms in their shop window, Mary became a member of Hornsea Golf Club in 1928.

Prior to this her father and mother, both well known members of the club, had encouraged Mary to take an interest in the game and it is reputed to have been the exhibition match between James Braid and Havers which first fired a real interest.

Always a strong competitor in club competitions Miss Johnson played in a number of national events for girls but undoubtedly her finest years were the early 1930s. In 1930 Mary started entering

*Receiving prizes for the Diamond Jubilee betterball competition.*
*Mrs. B. Smith, Mrs. G. Sedgewick, Mrs. B. Briggs, Mr. D. Roach.*

County senior events and did very creditably in the Yorkshire Championship meeting and reached the final of the Challenge Bowl, only losing at the 19th hole.

Two years later, at Moor Allerton in Leeds, Mary Johnson became the only lady member of Hornsea Golf Club to win the Yorkshire Ladies' Championship in its first 100 years.

Members back at Hornsea heard the news and an excited crowd of ladies decided to meet the new champion on the way home. Undecided

*Mary Johnson.*

*Welcoming home Mary Johnson, Yorkshire County Championship 1932.*
*From left: Queeny Todd (face in the corner), Mrs. Proctor, Miss Bess Cuttill,*
*Mary Johnson, Mrs. Frost, Miss Booth, Mrs. Blackmore.*

whether she would travel via Beverley or Skirlaugh they decided to wait at Sigglesthorne. The Johnson's car came into sight having come via York and Beverley with Mary's proud mother at the wheel.

Stopped by the welcoming party the vehicle was immediately decorated with balloons and flags and the Yorkshire champion, the first in Hornsea's history was escorted along the road to the Alexandra Hotel in Hornsea where a party had been arranged.

Mary defended her title in 1933 at Hallamshire Golf Club and again reached the final only to be beaten after a very hard match. But this year saw her reach the finals of the English Womens' Close Championship at Westward Ho, Devon, for the first time. She made a great impression on everybody who saw her by not only the quality of her golf but for her permanently sunny disposition. The eminent writer Henry Longhurst wrote at the time about her semi-final win, "Miss Johnson won by 5/4. She had played what was probably the best golf seen during the week, and I do not think that there was a woman in the world who could have beaten her."

Unfortunately she did not win the event but the directors of Hornsea Golf Club were so impressed by her achievements they made her an honorary life member.

Mary was a finalist in the Yorkshire County championship for five consecutive years between 1932 and 1936 and again won in 1934 at Hull Golf Club. She played for Yorkshire on 120 occasions, reached the final of the English Championship again in 1934 and represented England in the Home Internationals in 1934 and 1935. Many experienced observers considered she was very unlucky not to have been chosen to play in the inaugural and subsequent Curtis Cup matches against the U.S.A.

Mary Johnson went on to become Mrs. Toogood, moved away from Hornsea and sadly died a few years before this book was written.

The Hansons were another very well known family in Hornsea in the 1920s-30s. Colonel and Mrs. Hanson and their two daughters lived in Rolston Hall where the club benefactor Major Howarth Booth had resided prior to his death.

One of the Hanson girls was tragically killed in a riding accident but her sister Betty became an enthusiastic golfer and in 1928, together with a good number of other members, entered the Yorkshire Challenge Bowl which was held at Hornsea for the first time.

Betty was playing to a handicap of 20 and in the first competition of the meeting for the Victory Cup met the redoubtable Jean Rudgard from York who played off four. Betty lost 6 & 5.

In the knock-out stages of the main event, the Challenge Bowl itself, Betty Hanson reached the final and Jean Rudgard was again her opponent. Miss Rudgard's semi-final had been a marathon match against a Mrs. Bradshaw which unbelievably had only ended at the 44th hole! Twenty-six extra holes!!!

Doubtless this must have taxed the stamina of even a golfer of Jean Rudgard's legendary stamina. Nevertheless, as the final progressed she was two up with four holes to play against Hornsea's finalist. But Betty Hanson was determined not to be beaten and had squared the match by the eighteenth hole and proceeded to win the 19th. Hornsea club and its captain Tom Wells were delighted.

The year 1956 saw the Yorkshire Challenge Bowl competition return to Hornsea and again a large number of the local ladies entered the competition. Once again a local member was successful when Mary Kirkus, daughter of the redoubtable P.R. Davies won the final. The Yorkshire Challenge bowl competition is an extremely strenuous event which taxes not only golfing ability but also stamina. The winning competitor must first qualify and then play 36 holes of hard competitive golf over each of the following two days. Hornsea, with its length and comparatively heavy walking ground, is one of the sternest tests.

In 1979 two new lady members joined the club. Kathy and Penny Clarke were the wife and daughter of Tony

*Mary Kirkus.*

Clarke who had moved from South Wales to take up a position with the local Constabulary.

The two made their mark in their first year when Penny won the club Scratch Cup and her mother was runner up.

Penny Clarke was already a Welsh junior international golfer and had represented the first class county of Glamorgan at senior level prior to coming to Hornsea.

In 1979 Penny was a semi-finalist in the Yorkshire Championship played at Ganton and in the same year was selected to represent Yorkshire at County level. The following year she played at Moor Allerton in the Championship, forty-seven years after Mary

*Penny Clarke.*

61

Johnson had won the trophy there, and reached the final but sadly lost after an extremely hard match.

It was also in 1980 that she teamed up with Jane Rhodes of West Bowling. who had beaten her in the final of the County Championship and together they won the Northern Ladies' Foursomes played at Brough.

Penny's greatest honour was when she was selected to represent England in the home internationals in 1980.

Penny was a very popular member at Hornsea and, like Mary Johnson her prowess at the game sat very lightly on her shoulders. She was everybody's friend and on one occasion, when playing some of her best golf, turned out for the Hornsea Ladies Friendly Team when they were one short.

Moving away from Hornsea on her marriage, she currently lives in Somerset and work and two young daughters have prevented her playing much golf for a number of years.

Kathy Clarke.

Penny's mother Kathy, always a doughty competitor despite not taking up golf until 1970, won a number of competitions in Wales and in 1985 was runner-up in the Yorkshire Challenge Bowl at Hallowes Golf Club. The following year she went one better and won the trophy, this time at Bridlington Golf Club. The final and semi-final rounds were complete contrasts with Kathy playing some of her finest golf in the morning to overcome a very strong opponent. By the afternoon the strain was beginning to tell and a very tired Hornsea lady, who unknown to most of those present had been forced to play the whole competition with a back support, just managed to clinch the match on the nineteenth hole.

Hornsea Ladies have had some notable successes in team events over the years and although records are not precise they won a great victory in 1934 and the club presented the team with commemorative

*The winners of the Yorkshire 'A' Team final at Pike Hills in 1985.*
*Left to right: Kathy Clarke, Mabel Jackson, Anne Gaines,*
*Pam Hammersley, Carol Wood, Margaret Moore, Pat Biggs, Betty Smith,*
*Josie Clapperson, seated: Monica Major.*

brooches but one of the most exciting was in 1985 when they appeared in the 'A' Team finals of the County at Pike Hills Golf Club, York.

A good crowd of men and women supporters and "caddies" turned up from Hornsea and they and the team were delighted when the hard fought matches ended in Hornsea receiving the trophy.

At the time of writing this book a new young star has joined the club. Suzie Turner, doing 'A' Levels at Hymers College is naturally gifted at a number of sports and has been excelling at golf since a very young age.

Prior to moving to Hornsea she won both the Northern Girls under-16 and under-18 championships in 1994 and in 1996 won the Northern Schools championship.

A member of Yorkshire County 2nd team for a number of years she is also receiving English squad training. Who knows what this young lady may achieve after this book's completion.

*Suzie Turner.*

## Halfway House

Before leaving the Ladies Lounge, mention must be made of the Halfway House.

In the 1950s there was what can only be described as a hut by the side of the 9th green. The hut contained soft drinks and beer and members could pay 1/- for the key. Helping themselves they put the cost in an honesty book and were billed monthly. Unfortunately for whatever reason the records started to differ from the stock consumed, and so three lady members offered to staff the hut on Sundays only. Barbara Biggs, Joan French and Elsie Hammond took on

*The old halfway house with replacement behind it.*

task and as there were no facilities, each Sunday they drove up with water carriers, calor gas and the refreshments. It is recalled the men were very appreciative and the ladies were so plied with strong drinks they were fearful of driving back along the road and made their somewhat erratic way back to the club house via the course.

Eventually a proper halfway house was constructed and two non-playing members, Edie Glew and Rene Hague, helped by Margaret Taylor, took over. Water and power were laid on and Sunday mornings at the halfway house became a club tradition.

When Mrs. Glew moved from Hornsea the ladies section took over the running of the halfway house but eventually fear of mice and lack of adequate toilet facilities led to the club installing a modern building.

The profit from the venture has always been ploughed back into the club and course and currently the ladies are planning to purchase a Centenary Clock from the funds which will grace the top of the Professionals Shop from centenary year onwards.

*Left to right: Mrs. Kathleen Bullivant, Lady President,*
*Mrs. Bess Smith, Past Lady President.*

65

## Chapter 5
## Some Notable Members

It would be impossible to mention everyone who deserved to have special recognition in this book for the contribution they have made to Hornsea Golf Club. Some excelled at the game, some were great characters, many were both. But the club has survived not only by virtue of notable individuals but on the many who quietly remained in the background, enjoyed their golf, and supported the club through all its trials and tribulations. A few of the outstanding personalities from the club's first hundred years are recalled in this section.

Hornsea has produced its fair share of good men golfers and, over the years has attracted many from other local clubs who have come to Rolston Road course because of the challenge it presented to high quality players.

### R. H. (Hugh) Morfitt

Hugh joined Hornsea Golf Club in 1950 and reduced his handicap to Scratch in 1955. It was to be 15 years before his handicap was to move up again.

Altogether he played 95 times for the East Riding Golf Union and represented Yorkshire on 59 occasions. He won the East Yorkshire championship twice in 1956 and 1960

*Hugh Morfitt*

Now in his seventies, Hugh is still playing off a handicap of four in East Sussex.

### Richard Hutton.

In 1997, in the darkest recesses of the darkest cupboard in Hornsea Golf Club an unusual find was made. Mounted on a sizeable piece of

66

wood was a bronze cast of the head of a young man. Underneath was inscribed on a small brass plaque:

Richard Hutton
East Riding of Yorkshire Champion 1970
Winner of the George Henriques Salver for
the best gross score of an under 24 years old
competitor in the Brabazon Trophy

Records reveal that between 1968-70 Richard Hutton of Hornsea played for Yorkshire on ten occasions and that in 1968 he was runner up in the Yorkshire Championship.

He is remembered as being on the greenkeeping staff at Brough Golf Club and being unable to play there he joined Hornsea. An Irishman by birth and temperament few can now remember him. It is thought he may have become assistant professional somewhere but nobody has been found who can enlighten us.

From information received almost too late to be included in this book it appears that Richard Hutton now lives in Sweden and plays in European Senior Golf events including the 1997 British Senior Open at Royal Portrush.

*The plaque awarded to Richard Hutton.*

## D. C. Downs.

D. C. Downs of Hornsea is recorded as having played for Yorkshire in the 1930s and it is thought this may have been a Stewart Downs, a Solicitor practising in Hull who was a very good golfer playing at Hornsea at that time. Records have been unable to confirm this.

## A. R. Walker Jnr.

*Richard Walker*

Richard Walker is one of those who probably qualify as both a good golfer and a character of the club.

A keen and industrious member, Richard became a director in 1972 and vice chairman in 1986. For ten years from 1972 he was handicap and competition secretary and from 1983 he was chairman of the Greens Committee.

Always off low single figures Richard made over 90 appearances for the East Riding Union and was Captain from 1980-83. He was the county's amateur champion in 1976 and match play champion in 1978. He was honoured with the Presidency of the Union in 1982.

He emigrated with his family to Australia in 1990 but hopes to return for a visit in centenary year.

## A. Wright

A chemist by profession, Alan Wright is arguably the best man player at Hornsea Golf Club as the Centenary approaches.

Playing off Scratch or thereabouts he joined the club in the early 1980s and has regularly represented it in all the scratch team matches.

A prominent name in both East Riding and Yorkshire County golf, Alan has appeared in Yorkshire colours on thirty occasions. He has won the East Riding Alliance championship on three occasions in 1983-84 and in 1991, the East Riding Open also on three occasions and has won the George Ashe Trophy five times.

In 1997, as this book is being written he achieved possibly his greatest success to date when at Moor Allerton on the 18th June he won the Yorkshire Stroke Play Championship with rounds of 70, 72. This is the first occasion that this comparatively new event has been won by a Hornsea player.

*Alan Wright and Paul Binnington.*

## P. R. Binnington

Paul is the son of two ex captains of the club, John and Pauline Binnington and he took to golf at an early age.

He won the Yorkshire Youths' Championship in 1988 and 1989 and played for Yorkshire on seven occasions at senior level. At the time although still a Hornsea member he was playing in Ganton colours.

Paul has now joined the Professional ranks and works at a local golf club.

## The Golf Teams

Hornsea have always prided themselves on fielding strong teams in the area's scratch leagues and their successes have been too numerous to set out here. Suffice to say they have somewhat dominated the East Riding competitions in recent years and only recently have they failed to retain their place in the Yorkshire First Division.

## Current Course Record

The record for the best round of golf under competitive conditions, on the newly reconstructed course, is held by C. J. Waite.

Chris Waite has been coming to Hornsea Golf Club since he was

*Chris Waite.*
*Holder of Hornsea Course Record in 1997.*

a toddler caddying for his father. His work has probably prevented him from reaching his full potential but he has represented the East Riding on numerous occasions and must be on the border of full Yorkshire honours. His record card in the Jack Major Trophy in 1994 was despite managing a five on the par 3 twelfth hole.

## Major Howarth-Booth

Little is known about his prowess at golf but one of the men who played an absolutely crucial role in Hornsea Golf Club's development in the early years was Major Howarth Booth. Without his generous interest and help it is unlikely the course would have been where it is today.

| COMPETITION | *J.MAJOR TROPHY* | | | | | | | Please indicate which tee used | |
|---|---|---|---|---|---|---|---|---|---|
| DATE *3·9·94* | | TIME | | | | Handicap | Strokes Rec'd | PAR 72 SSS 72 | |
| Player A | *C.J.Waite* | | | | | *2* | | PAR 72 SSS 71 | |
| Player B | | | | | | | | | |

| Hole | Marker's Score | Name | White Yards | Par | Yellow Yards | Stroke Index | Score A | B | W = + L = – H = 0 POINTS | Stroke Index |
|---|---|---|---|---|---|---|---|---|---|---|
| 1 | | Crab Apple | 326 | 4 | 311 | 16 | 3 | | | 13 |
| 2 | | Ditch | 333 | 4 | 322 | 14 | 3 | | | 11 |
| 3 | | Dog Leg | 498 | 5 | 497 | 6 | 5 | | | 3 |
| 4 | | Gate | 397 | 4 | 387 | 4 | 5 | | | 9 |
| 5 | | Whins | 304 | 4 | 304 | 18 | 3 | | | 15 |
| 6 | | Tower | 448 | 4 | 445 | 2 | 4 | | | 5 |
| 7 | | Grouse | 191 | 3 | 162 | 10 | 5 | | | 17 |
| 8 | | Seaward | 508 | 5 | 498 | 12 | 4 | | | 1 |
| 9 | | Halfway House | 409 | 4 | 391 | 7 | 4 | | | 7 |
| | | OUT | 3414 | 37 | 3317 | | 36 | | | |

| 10 | | Down Hill | 420 | 4 | 405 | 5 | 4 | | | 4 |
| 11 | | Pond | 291 | 4 | 281 | 15 | 4 | | | 12 |
| 12 | | Basin | 175 | 3 | 160 | 13 | 2 | | | 16 |
| 13 | | Hedge | 349 | 4 | 340 | 11 | 4 | | | 14 |
| 14 | | Furze | 470 | 4 | 460 | 1 | 4 | | | 2 |
| 15 | | Hummocks | 450 | 4 | 440 | 3 | 4 | | | 8 |
| 16 | | Himalayas | 533 | 5 | 479 | 8 | 4 | | | 6 |
| 17 | | Rolston Dip | 172 | 3 | 159 | 17 | 4 | | | 18 |
| 18 | | Home | 411 | 4 | 399 | 9 | 4 | | | 10 |

| | STABLEFORD POINTS OR PAR RESULT | IN | 3271 | 35 | 3123 | | 32 | | | |
| | | OUT | 3414 | 37 | 3317 | | 36 | | | |
| | | TOTAL | 6685 | 72 | 6440 | | 68 | | | |
| Copyright Eagle Promotions Ltd 0883-344244 | | HANDICAP | | | | | 2 | | Holes won ............... | |
| | | NETT | | | | | 66 | | Holes lost ............... | |
| | | | | | | | | | Result ............... | |

Markers Signature *P.W.Atkin*        Players Signature *C.J. Waite*

*Current Course Record*

*Some good scores over the years.*

*Some good scores over the years.*

*Mr. B. B. Haworth-Booth, D.L., J.P.*

Benjamin Blades Howarth Booth was a member of a long established family with, as his second forename denotes, connections with the famous Blades family of Hull, entrepreneurs. Their main residence was Hullbank Hall, Hull which still stands today between Beverley Road and the river Hull.

Rolston or Rowlston Hall came into the family when William Brough, Marshall of the Admiralty, who owned the house, married a Mrs. Brough about the end of the eighteenth century. When Mrs. Brough died the house passed to her niece Theresa Arneman who was the grandmother of Benjamin Blades Howarth. He later added Booth to his surname.

The story is told that William Brough lived in the Hall which was formerly moated and was entrusted with the suppression of piracy along the east coast. One famous freebooter, Paul Jones, is reputed never to have sailed past Rowlston without firing his cannon at the Hall to show his contempt for his adversary!

Major Booth, born in London on new year's day in 1857 was educated at Eton and Trinity College, Cambridge.

In the county during the first two decades of the twentieth century he was a member of the landed gentry, a Justice of the Peace and a

Deputy Lieutenant of the County. His love of the game of golf was very much to the benefit of Hornsea Golf Club is recorded elsewhere in this book.

**P. R. Davies; Peter Ramsden and Tommy Wells**

This triumverate was pretty well all powerful at Hornsea Golf Club during the late 1920s and the 1930s.

Percy Randolph Davies was arguably the single most influential individual in the club. Chairman of the Board in 1932-33 he was also Captain in the latter year. He remained on the Board

*P. R. Davies.*

of Directors for many years and loved the game of golf and Hornsea Golf Club.

Known to one and all as P.R.D. he owned clothing shops in Hull and Sheffield which were named PRDS. He was one of the regular commuters on the Hornsea-Hull railway.

His daughter Mary was a long serving member of the club and was Lady President for many years. She was an honorary life member of the club.

Peter Ramsden was for many years Chairman of the Hornsea Board of Directors. Not only was he a keen and enthusiastic member of the club but being Manager of the local branch of the Midland Bank was absolutely crucial in trying to see the club through its financial traumas. His name is perpetuated on the Holmes/Ramsden trophy, played for every year.

Tom Wells belonged to a local family associated with Hornsea Golf Club from its inception. Auctioneers in Southgate he was club captain in 1928. A good golfer he was known as an extremely dapper and well-dressed member of the club.

**Tim Tomlinson**

Soon after Tim joined the Golf Club in 1937 he was taken off to War and as Captain Tomlinson of the RAOC was reputed to have

*Tim Tomlinson*

successfully misdirected most of the stores destined for the British Eighth Army to various sleazy merchants in Egypt. That at least is the story Tim would tell against himself!! In his latter years he used to winter in the Canary Islands and not being able to sleep would sit in his bedroom at night and write cards to his cronies back at the club. They all carried an identical message starting with "Am sitting on the patio in the blazing sun gently sipping a gin and tonic...."

But the leg pulling and fun loving side of Tim masked a much more serious and astute business man. Joint Managing Director of Hull based Lincoln & Hull Water Transport Co. Ltd., he became the then youngest director of Hornsea Golf Club in 1946. He was chairman of the Greens' Committee for 18 years until he became Chairman of the club in 1966.

Tim was club captain in 1960 and always one for new ventures started a Sunday 'top dogs' competition to see who were the best pair of golfers in 4-ball play. The idea was to mix members and get them out of the rut of playing in the same four-ball every week. Eric Dyson, his vice captain had a pair of silver dog badges made to be worn by the current top dogs when playing each week. Although the competition as such no longer exists the practice of mixing fours on a Sunday continues.

Tim was also responsible for starting the Elderly Gentlemens' Golfing Society about which more is written elsewhere in this book.

In his latter years Tim moved to a bungalow overlooking the 18th fairway and when he died the club lost a great servant and a tremendous character.

## E. L. Biggs

The late Ted Biggs was Captain of Hornsea in 1959. A District Valuer working for the Inland Revenue in Hull he was an enthusiastic member of the club for many years.

Ted has no great claim to being picked out for special mention except for one thing. A number of members who knew have expressed the opinion to the writer that without any reflection on any other club captain, Ted sticks in their minds as being one of the nicest men ever to have had that honour.

*E. L. Biggs.*

## Jack Major

Known fondly as Mr. Golf in his latter days at the club, Jack Major was Chairman of the Board, Secretary and Treasurer all rolled into one when he tragically died while playing the course on 22nd August 1986. He was 57 years old.

Orphaned as a child when his mother was killed in an accident and his father died shortly afterwards, Jack went to Read's School where he immediately showed his prowess as a sportsman. He played schoolboy representative football and as

*Jack Major.*

soon as he was old enough he joined the famous Bishop Auckland amateur football club and represented them during their golden years after the Second World War.

75

He captained the team and appeared three times at Wembley in the Cup Final. An RAF PTI during national service he represented the Royal Air Force and played a number of times for England.

He married Monica in 1959 and signed semi-professional forms for Hull City. He even played one season for Roubaix in the French first division.

Having joined a Hull firm of accountants and being persuaded to take up golf he went for lessons to Reg Wood in Pryme Street. He never played football again but became immersed in the game of golf. He and his wife joined Hornsea Golf club during the Suez crisis and within six months Mr. Irvine the Hon. treasurer of the club, had persuaded Jack to take over that role in his place.

Playing to low single figures possibly his greatest achievement was when he qualified for the Brabazon Trophy.

Even more important than any golfing achievements was the work he did in administering the club. It would not be an over-statement to say that he virtually ran Hornsea Golf Club for many years. When he died so suddenly the club was forced to quickly readjust to fill the many gaps he left behind.

He was sadly missed as a great sportsman and gentleman.

*Jimmy Kidd.*

### James V. Kidd

Jimmy, who was born in Bridlington in 1910 has been a golfer all his life and still does his regular eighteen holes, albeit in a buggy, as this book is written.

Like so many others possibly his best golfing years were lost to the War because in 1939 he was playing in the Bridlington team which consisted of:

T. J. Thirsk, handicap +2 a regular English international and winner of the Hitler Trophy at the 1936 Berlin Olympic Games held in Baden Baden. Because of his outstanding achievements Mr. Thirsk was made honorary member of many Yorkshire Golf Clubs including Hornsea.

76

J. A. Stout, handicap +2 Many times an English international and winner of the English closed championship and member of the Walker Cup side against America.

R. H. Romyn handicap 2.

J. V. Kidd handicap 1

In 1950 Jimmy moved his work to Hull and joined Hornsea Golf Club where he formed an enduring friendship and golf partnership with O. T. (Terry) Hall. They played hundreds of games together over 44 years until Terry's untimely death.

Captain of Hornsea in 1956 he was made Captain of Captains of the Hull and District Golf Captains Association in 1966.

Jimmy had a reputation for working and playing hard and his capacity for the social life is already part of Hornsea Golf Club's folk lore.

### Jack Hardy

Jack may be a slightly controversial entry in this section because he is a comparatively new member of the club. The writer will however make no apologies for putting him in, firstly because he plays golf with him every Saturday, and secondly and much more importantly because Jack has a claim to fame in Hornsea Golf Club never before equalled and unlikely to be so in the future.

He became Captain of Hornsea Golf Club in his 77th year, when most are considering doing a quiet thirteen holes or buying a buggy, Jack Hardy ran

*Jack Hardy.*

as busy and entertaining a year as anyone less than half his age.

Jack with his wife Amy moved to Hornsea in 1983 and he became Captain ten years later. No stranger to some of life's slings and arrows he desires and often achieves 100% perfection in everything he undertakes. His sometimes compulsive irascibility is more than

77

offset by a beguiling sense of humour. Golf is his absorbing interest and his amazing fitness for his age seems to allow him to play at least four times every week.

An amazing person and long may he grace the Hornsea course.

### Claude Lax

The major part of this record of Hornsea Golf Club's first hundred years is being written in 1997 and at that time Claude Lax had been a member for 70 years. Son of a well known former Secretary of the club and two brothers and a sister playing the game Claude joined on 27th December 1927 at the age of 18 years.

He was Captain in 1948 and because of sickness in the family of his vice-captain he decided not to stand down for another year until his successor could take over the role.

In 1997 Claude is still in very good health and is regularly out on the course, and has been made an Honorary Life Member of the club to mark his 70th year of membership.

*Claude Lax.*

## Chapter 6
## SOCIETIES AT HORNSEA
### The Scorpions
by John Smallwood — The 'President'

The Scorpions were founded in 1933, the original idea for what was to become a club institution being put forward by T. S. Holyman or Sid to his friends. Sid had difficulty in always getting a four-ball together and eventually he, and a few others decided to form a group to overcome this problem. It was thought it would also facilitate the integration of new members in the club.

The founder members of The Scorpions were:-

| | | |
|---|---|---|
| O. R. W. Agerskow | B. Edwards | C. H. Lax |
| F. Butler | D. Ferraby | H. A. Lax |
| C. R. Clarke | S. G. French | H. M. Lumley |
| R. H. Clay | A. Havercroft | R. Pinchon |
| H. L. Collinson | T. Holyman | A. Scholey |
| R. G. Collinson | R. Kershaw | A. H. Stones |
| G. A. Dick | A. F. H. Lax | N. H. Taylor |
| G. A. Dosser | A. L. Lax | S. Woodhouse |

It will be seen that the Lax family made a substantial contribution to the numbers of the original group.

The origins of the name Scorpion is a little uncertain but is believed to have been devised from a slight revision of the expression 'The sting is in the tale'.

A badge was drawn by Alf Dick, a draughtsman with Metalbox and he designed and drew a crest showing a bird(ie); an eagle; a scorpion; a tiger and a rabbit. The reasons for the first three are clear and the last two are assumed to denote those who were good golfers and the 'others'. The motto beneath the crest reads 'The sting is in the tales they tell'.

Since its inception the Scorpions has continued with only a brief respite during the Second World War. Apart from the camaraderie and enjoyable golf the principle reason for the Scorpions has always been to help new members assimilate into the club. There are

79

twenty-four Scorpions who play together every other Sunday between October and March. The format is four-ball better ball and competition is on a league basis.

The league winners are awarded the Scorpions League Cup and a cash prize just large enough to buy the invited guests a drink. Presentations are made at the Annual Dinner which is attended by both past and present members of the group.

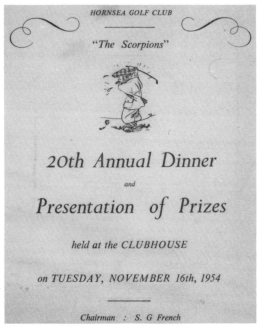

HORNSEA GOLF CLUB

"The Scorpions"

## 20th Annual Dinner

*and*

## Presentation of Prizes

held at the CLUBHOUSE

on TUESDAY, NOVEMBER 16th, 1954

Chairman : S. G French

The dinner is generally a hilarious affair with a great many stories and very old jokes being told. One of the traditional highlights of the evening is a ritual slaughtering of the world famous 'Rum Titty' song. This is a rather tasteful lament of unknown origin although widely thought to have been written by a two-year old dyslexic, such is the profound nature of the lyrics.

Other events of the season include a match against Withernsea on a home and away basis for the Seaside Cup, while a major highlight every year is the Scorpions Cup Competition. The prize for this Stableford competition is the honour of keeping and cleaning the enormous trophy. The cleaning alone is claimed to be a major drain on household finances and needless to say it is won every year with a very mediocre score.

The Scorpions outing is another annual event generally held in early May. It always attracts a good turnout of about twenty members who squeeze themselves into miscellaneous vehicles and retire to a distant golf course for an extremely long weekend. It involves late nights and very protracted games of snooker into the small hours followed by too much golf. The main event is generally won by the Scorpion with the hardiest constitution.

One final event organised by the Scorpions is the annual exchange with Scarborough North Cliff Golf Club which is now thrown open to all members and is very well attended.

The Scorpions have always supported the club in the broadest sense of the word. They were founded as an integral part of Hornsea Golf Club, are not a splinter group or an elitist crowd and always have the club's best interests at heart. In the past two years they have organised social events and contributed significant sums to the Centenary Fund. More recently, the new trophy cabinet which resides in the spike bar has been funded by the Scorpions.

Scorpions go from strength to strength and it is hoped they will continue to do so and continue in the same spirit they have enjoyed for the last sixty-five years.

### The ACWACS

Not wishing to get quite as committed as The Scorpions during the summer of 1970, a conversation took place at the club between Jack Major and his Sunday partner Laurie Dexter, about Sunday golf in the winter. It was decided to try and get a group of players together to play a competition between themselves.

Stalwarts such as Brian Falkingham, Ken Taylor, Mike Hesk and Reg Wood were all in favour and a group of twelve was formed. At the time of the discussion on the subject someone was heard to remark, "Oh another club within a club!" and this chance remark was seized upon to arrive at the ACWAC.

Others in the first group included John King, Ken Brown, Hugh Morfitt, Mike Markham, Ricky Hunt and Mike Blackburn.

Competitions were Better Ball Stablefords, everyone playing with a different partner each week and the scores being recorded individually to form a league table. Competition was keen although not too serious and the friendly spirit engendered in the group has continued to this day.

Every season ends with a Dinner at Luigi's Restaurant attended by wives and girlfriends. The meal concludes with speeches by the top and bottom players of the year's league and the top player receives a pewter tankard donated by John King. The bottom man originally received a plastic chamber pot. The cup is still awarded today but sadly the chamber pot has mysteriously vanished from the scene.

The year preceding the centenary year saw sixteen players still enjoying the fun of being a member of Hornsea ACWACS.

## The Elderly Gentlemen's Golfing Society

The idea of a golfing society for retired golfers did not originate in Hornsea Golf Club but was the idea of Olly Gay, the then President of the Hessle Golf Club in the 1970s. He felt many members of golf clubs who retired from work in their sixties felt rather outside their club's main competitive activities. This was specially so in relation to inter-club games.

Mr. Gay contacted other clubs in the area and six expressed an interest. Hornsea did not. The six clubs arranged to play semi-competitive matches on a home and away basis followed by a drink and snack in the club house. They called themselves The Retired Gentlemen's Golfing Society.

The system was a success and on 20th April 1983 some twenty members of Hornsea club met to discuss joining the arrangement. They decided to call themselves The Elderley Gentlemen's Golfing Society (EGGS) and Tim Tomlinson, a prime mover in the matter, was elected the first President. The first Captain was Tommy Dunn, his Vice Captain was Claud Varley and Frank Knott was the original Secretary. Fixtures with other clubs were arranged and the Hornsea EGGS were off the ground.

The rules are simple — members must be 60 years old or more, retired from their main work and teams are selected in order to give everyone roughly the same number of games in matches each season. In addition to the inter-club matches three cups have been donated for the Hornsea Eggs to compete for.

Inter-club match results are never announced publicly to avoid any suggestion of one club being better than another.

More and more golf clubs in the area have been desirous of joining the EGGS circuit but in 1984 it was decided Hornsea could accept no more fixtures in deference to other demands on the course.

Running now since 1983 the EGGS have provided a great deal of golfing pleasure to members and has been responsible for many friendships being developed. Long may this happiness for the more mature gentlemen members continue!

**The 77 Plus Club**

*1991 Raising of the flags for the '77' Club.*
*Left to right: Peter Drinkall, David Deacon, Brian Kirton.*

This is arguably the most unusual of the little sections within Hornsea Golf Club.

Not content with the Elderley Gentlemen's Golfing Society (EGGS) the club has a select number eligible to join a group of those still playing over 77 years of age.

It started as a joke in 1988 when Jimmy Kidd saw a number of golfers gathered in black caps and pink sweaters and on enquiring was told they called themselves the 'Hornsea Splinters'. Not to be outdone Jimmy decided to form the 77 Plus Club with the rules being that members had to be over 77 and still capable of playing a full round of golf.

Jimmy elected himself Chairman and appointed Claud Lax to be Secretary.

Since that time the club has run an annual AM-AM event with the numbers swelled by a number of honorary officials who have yet to reach 77 years, plus invited guests.

Perhaps of all the clubs within the club this one is likely to have a fluctuating membership but the numbers have consistently grown and at the time of writing this book had grown from the original two members to fourteen.

*Senior members of the original 77+ Club*
*Left to right: Steve Roberts, Claud Lax, Jimmy Kidd, Tim Tomlinson,*
*Fred Hampton, Jim Geddes.*

## Chapter 7
## Club Professionals

Records are somewhat scarce about exact dates that professionals were engaged. Originally they were expected to have wives who would become steward/caretakers of the club and until the late 1970s were also responsible for greenkeeping.

| | | | |
|---|---|---|---|
| 1898-1901 W. Dell | | 1929-1939 S. Stenhouse | |
| 1901-1906 W. Finch | | (called up for military service) | |
| 1906-1913 F. Wingate | | 1946-1947 S. Stenhouse | |
| 1913-1919 L. G. White | | 1947-1948 G. N. White | |
| 1919-1920 | Boyd | 1948-1951 S. McDowell | |
| 1920-1921 | McLaughlin | 1951-1954 T. G. Bielby | |
| 1921-1926 J. Dailey | | 1954-1978 | P. Wright |
| 1926-1929 R. Whiting | | 1978- | B. Thompson |

The sensible idea that the wife of the Professional/Greenkeeper should be the stewardess ran into some difficulties from the early days.

In 1920 the Boyd's marriage foundered and he left but she remained as stewardess and a Mr. McLaughlin was appointed temporary professional. When Mrs. Boyd left in 1921 the club appointed a Mrs. Armitage at £1.1s.0d. per week plus free board and lodging.

The situation was not satisfactory however and Mr. and Mrs. Dailey were appointed as professional and stewardess respectively.

Dailey ran into serious trouble and was given the opportunity of resigning or face the sack in 1926. His plea for a second chance was rejected and he left. On appointment of Mr. and Mrs. Whiting from Hanger Lane Golf Club Ealing the club decided to make Mrs. Armitage redundant.

Unfortunately for her this was somewhat premature because Mrs. Whiting proved to be quite useless as a caterer and eventually the cooking was let to a Mr. Hockney.

The Whiting's were dismissed in 1929 and the tradition of routinely employing married couples as Professional and Steward/Caretaker ceased.

# Hornsea Golf Club.

# HOUSE TARIFF.

| | | |
|---|---|---|
| Cold Lunch: | Joint, Vegetables, Sweets, Bread, Cheese and Biscuits | 3/- |
| „ „ | Joint, Vegetable, Bread, Cheese and Biscuits | 2/6 |
| „ „ | Plate of Meat, Vegetables and Bread | 2/- |
| Chop or Steak and Vegetable, Bread, Cheese and Biscuits (to order) | | 3/- |

By arrangement with Mrs. Armitage.   Two Hours' Notice required.
NOT supplied during Week-ends nor Bank Holidays.

| | | | |
|---|---|---|---|
| Sandwich | | Large 1/- | Small 6d. |
| Pot of Tea, Bread and Butter and One Egg, or Jam and Cake | | | 1/- |
| Cup of Coffee, or Cocoa | | | 4d. |
| „ Tea | | | 3d. |
| Glass of Milk | | | 3d. |

**TABLE MONEY.**

Luncheons   2d. per person.   ::   Teas   1d. per person.

---

| SPIRITS & LIQUEURS. | per glass | | BEER (in Bottle). | per bot |
|---|---|---|---|---|
| Scotch Whisky | 10d | | Bass's Pale Ale | 8½d |
| „ „ and Syphon | 1/- | | Guinness's Stout | 8½d |
| Brandy | 1/1 | | | |
| Gin and Bitters | 10d | | Draught Bitter Beer   pint | 10d |
| Sherry and Bitters | 10d | | „ „ half-pint | 5½d |
| Port Wine | 10d | | | |
| Cherry Brandy | 10d | | **MINERALS.** | per bot |
| Cherry Whisky | 10d | | Large Schweppes Soda | 7d |
| Creme de Menthe | 10d | | Small „ „ | 5d |
| Benedictine | 1/6 | | „ Malvern Water | 5d |
| Gin and Vermouth, large | 1/- | | „ Dry Ginger Ale | 5d |
| „ „ small | 9d | | Lemonade, Ginger Beer | 4d |

---

| TOBACCO. | | | CIGARETTES. | | | |
|---|---|---|---|---|---|---|
| 2-oz. Three Nuns | 2/5 | | 50 Three Castles | | | 3/4 |
| 1-oz. „ „ | 1/2½ | | 20 „ „ | Machine Made | | 1/4 |
| 1-oz. Smith's Glasgow | | | 20 „ „ | Hand Made | | 1/6 |
| Mixture | 1/- | | 10 „ „ | | | 8d |
| 1-oz. Country Life | 1/- | | 50 Gold Flake | | | 2/6 |
| 1-oz. Waverley Mixture | 1/- | | 20 „ | | | 1/- |
| | | | 10 „ | | | 6d |
| 2-oz. Foursome Mixture | 2/2 | | 20 Greys | | | 1/6 |
| 1-oz. „ „ | 1/1 | | 10 Myrtle Brand, etc | | | 6d |

The Committee requests that Members and Visitors will pay for all Drinks when the Chit is presented.

However, the year 1946 saw the usual problems with Stewards. Mr. and Mrs. Pinder were appointed but were dismissed within a few months — Mrs. Pinder being allowed to stay on provided her husband had no contact whatsoever with the club.

For most of the club's early history the professional in post assumed responsibility for the greenkeeping and the staff. This ceased when Mr. Stenhouse took charge in 1929 and long serving Donkin took on the role of greenkeeper. When he eventually finished in 1953 the then professional T. G. Bielby was asked to resume responsibility for the greens. Percy Wright carried on the tradition which ceased when Brian Thompson took over and Roger Bielby was made greenkeeper, a post later renamed as Course Manager.

Amazingly since 1929 Stan Stenhouse, Percy Wright and Brian Thompson have, between them, served the club for a total of fifty-three years as club professionals.

## Stan Stenhouse

When Whiting was dismissed in 1929, Ferraday, his initial replacement only stayed a few days and Stan Stenhouse, assistant professional at Kirkella approached the club to see if he could have the job. After playing a trial round of golf with P. R. Davies, Peter Ramsden and Tom Wells he was offered the position.

Percy Wright was then the assistant professional at Hornsea and Stenhouse asked him to arrange 'digs' as he was to start work in a week's time. When Stan arrived for work Percy had to report he had been unable to find accommodation but said he could stay with his 'mum' at the bakery on the corner of Eastgate and Cliff Road in Hornsea. So the new professional joined the Wrights who had four girls and four boys out of their family of ten, still living at home. He was never to leave the comforts of the Wright's home for the eleven years he stayed at Hornsea and this despite the family moving house on two occasions.

Stan played in the British Open Championship at least eight times and played with all the top golfers of the day. Possibly his best golfing years were lost to the War from which he returned in 1946 staying in Hornsea for just one year before leaving the club to become the profesional at Hull Golf Club in 1947.

Stan is an honorary life member of Hornsea Golf Club.

*Three long serving Professionals. Left to right: Brian Thompson, Stan Stenhouse, Percy Wright.*

## Percy Wright

Percy Wright served a long apprenticeship of nine years as assistant professional at Hornsea Golf Club starting in the mid-1920s. He then became the professional at Leyburn and Catterick Garrison clubs respectively before being called up in 1939.

Captured in the North African desert he served three years as a prisoner-of-war in Germany where to the astonishment of his guards he started golf lessons with a begged club and ball.

Always keen to return to Hornsea, when the post became vacant in 1954 he applied, was appointed and remained until his retirement in 1978.

Like Stan, Percy was also honoured by being made an honorary life member of the club when he left.

## Brian Thompson

Percy, Stan Stenhouse and the current professional Brian Thompson have together served the club for a total of 54 years, well over half of its existence.

Coming from a golfing family Brian Thompson won the Midland Assistants' Championship in the 1960s, won the Lord Derby's Match Play Championship in 1973 and the Yorkshire Open Championship in 1982.

Before replacing Percy Wright in 1978 he had been the Lincolnshire Open Champion in 1968-72-74.

A very good golfer who is reticent about discussing his achievement he almost discounts the fact that since coming to Hornsea he has reached the final stages of the British Open Championship with an extremely creditable 30th place finish on one occasion. This was in the period when the 'British' was completely dominated by overseas entrants and merely to qualify to play was a great achievement.

He continues to play good golf and has developed into a first class teacher much sought after by golfers from a wide area.

## Club Secretaries

Like some of the details about the club professionals and stewards the facts about club secretaries are somewhat difficult to confirm, particularly as far as dates are concerned.

The following gives a list of Secretaries of the golf club in what is believed to be chronological order and with dates or presumed dates where possible.

| 1898 | W. Minnett Good |
|------|-----------------|
| 1899 | R. P. Maw |
| 1907 | W. Rutter Smith |
| 1910 | T. Wells |
| 1915 | W. E. Hay |
| 1920 | W. P. Murdoch |
| | J. Fletcher |
| | Horsley |
| 1936 | A. F. H. Lax |
| | H. L. McIntosh |
| | A. Renshaw |
| | A. Bowden |
| | J. L. Major |
| 1986 | B. Kirton |

Brian Kirton was appointed as the first, full time, salaried secretary of Hornsea Golf Club, when he retired from personnel work at BP Raglan Bay in South Wales and returned to live in East Yorkshire. A keen golfer and a sound administrator he has been a great acquisition for the club.

*Brian Kirton.*

# Appendix 1
## Chairmen of the Board

| | | | | |
|---|---|---|---|---|
| 1920 | H. E. Kirbus | | 1958 | R. G. Collinson |
| 1921 | H. A. Learoyd | | 1959 | E. L. Biggs |
| 1922 | " " | | 1960 | C. Cartledge |
| 1923 | " " | | 1961 | " " |
| 1924 | " " | | 1962 | " " |
| 1925 | " " | | 1963 | " " |
| 1926 | " " | | 1964 | R. M. Roach |
| 1927 | " " | | 1965 | " " |
| 1928 | " " | | 1966 | T. Tomlinson |
| 1929 | J. H. Tate | | 1967 | " " |
| 1930 | " " | | 1968 | R. S. F. Brown |
| 1931 | " " | | 1969 | N. P. Seaton |
| 1932 | R. P. J. Davies | | 1970 | " " |
| 1933 | " " | | 1971 | " " |
| 1934 | W. Cutting | | 1972 | " " |
| 1935 | " " | | 1973 | " " |
| 1936 | P. H. R. Ramsden | | 1974 | " " |
| 1937 | " " | | 1975 | " " |
| 1938 | " " | | 1976 | " " |
| 1939 | " " | | 1977 | " " |
| 1940 | " " | | 1978 | " " |
| 1941 | " " | | 1979 | " " |
| 1942 | " " | | 1980 | " " |
| 1943 | " " | | 1981 | J. L. Major |
| 1944 | " " | | 1982 | " " |
| 1945 | " " | | 1983 | " " |
| 1946 | " " | | 1984 | " " |
| 1947 | W. Singleton | | 1985 | " " |
| 1948 | " " | | 1986 | " " |
| 1949 | " " | | 1986/7 | B. Falkingham |
| 1950 | " " | | 1988 | " " |
| 1951 | " " | | 1989 | " " |
| 1952 | D. Ferraby | | 1990 | " " |
| 1953 | " " | | 1991 | " " |
| 1954 | " " | | 1992 | " " |
| 1955 | R. G. Collinson | | 1993 | " " |
| 1956 | " " | | 1994 | " " |
| 1957 | " " | | 1994/7 | S. L. Wright |

91

# Appendix 2
## Captains

| | | | |
|---|---|---|---|
| 1898 | T. Gregory | 1936 | D. Hitchins |
| 1899 | " " | 1937 | D. Ferraby |
| 1900 | T. B. Holmes | 1938 | A. H. Stones |
| 1901 | " " | 1939 | H. M. Lumley |
| 1902 | W. M. Good | 1940 | F. W. Harrison |
| 1903 | J. Fleming | 1041 | T. S. Holyman |
| 1904 | F. S. Brodrick | 1942-1944 | War |
| 1905 | H. A. Learoyd | 1945 | I. D. McIntyre |
| 1906 | " " | 1946 | " " |
| 1907 | R. P. Maw | 1947 | W. E. Naylor |
| 1908 | " " | 1948 | C. H. Lax |
| 1909 | " " | 1949 | " " |
| 1910 | R. Liversedge | 1950 | D. P. Shackles |
| 1911 | R. Reynolds | 1951 | W. E. Donnison |
| 1912 | " " | 1952 | E. L. Biggs |
| 1913 | " " | 1953 | T. E. Cassels |
| 1914 | C. H. Loncaster | 1954 | A. Renshaw |
| 1915 | " " | 1955 | O. T. Hall |
| 1916 | " " | 1956 | J. V. Kidd |
| 1917 | H. E. Holmes | 1957 | H. S. Biggs |
| 1918 | " " | 1958 | R. M. Roach |
| 1919 | " " | 1959 | E. G. Ashton |
| 1920 | H. E. Kirkus | 1960 | T. Tomlinson |
| 1921 | " " | 1961 | F. Dyson |
| 1922 | P. H. R. Ramsden | 1962 | R. S. F. Brown |
| 1923 | R. P. J. Davies | 1963 | J. L. Major |
| 1924 | J. H. Tate | 1964 | W. E. Eggleston |
| 1925 | C. Sutton | 1965 | J. T. Ashton |
| 1926 | A. E. Havercroft | 1966 | S. Sharp |
| 1927 | P. S. Hornsby | 1967 | N. P. Seaton |
| 1928 | T. Wells | 1968 | J. D. Thompson |
| 1929 | C. Shackles | 1969 | J. R. Busfield |
| 1930 | W. Cutting | 1970 | R. H. Hindle |
| 1931 | F. Butler | 1971 | J. E. Glew |
| 1932 | N. Allen | 1972 | M. Hesk |
| 1933 | A. J. Downs | 1973 | K. S. Brown |
| 1934 | W. M. McNicol | 1974 | W. Branton |
| 1935 | A. S. Pratt | 1975 | K. Busby |

| | | | |
|---|---|---|---|
| 1976 | J. R. Binnington | 1987 | R. H. Allen |
| 1977 | N. Schofield | 1988 | F. D. Jordan |
| 1978 | J. A. Scott | 1989 | K. Gorton |
| 1979 | M. R. Griffiths | 1990 | R. A. Wrigglesworth |
| 1980 | C. S. Roberts | 1991 | T. A. Williams |
| 1981 | B. Stevenson | 1992 | B. Farley |
| 1982 | J. F. Hammersley | 1993 | J. Hardy |
| 1983 | G. Appleton | 1994 | J. E. Bickenson |
| 1984 | F. Palin | 1995 | P. F. Slaven |
| 1985 | I. MacKechnie | 1996 | D. V. Hodgson |
| 1986 | R. Ducker | 1997 | J. R. Matthews |

## Appendix 3
## Lady Presidents

1920  Mrs. Haworth Booth
1937  Mrs. S. Earle
1945  Mrs. S. Holmes
1949  Mrs. I. Hanson
1955  Mrs. N. Johnson
1960  Mrs. P. Earle
1977  Mrs. H. H. Kirkus
1982  Mrs. L. E. Smith
1995  Mrs. C. Bullivant

# Appendix 4
## Lady Captains

| | | | |
|---|---|---|---|
| 1918 | Mrs. Stanley Earle | 1962 | Mrs. P. G. Leonard |
| 1919 | Mrs. Holmes | 1963 | Mrs. F. H. Smith |
| 1920 | Mrs. Alexander | 1964 | Mrs. F. Dyson |
| 1921 | Mrs. Stanley Earle | 1965 | Mrs. H. R. Coursh |
| 1922 | Mrs. Stanley Earle | 1966 | Miss E. Hammond |
| 1923 | Mrs. Hanson | 1967 | Mrs. W. Marshall |
| 1924 | Mrs. Holmes | 1968 | Mrs. K. C. Taylor |
| 1925 | Mrs. Mann | 1969 | Mrs. J. L. Major |
| 1926 | Mrs. Craft | 1970 | Mrs. J. R. Busfield |
| 1927 | Mrs. Holmes | 1971 | Mrs. B. Fenton |
| 1928 | Mrs. F. Wellstead | 1972 | Mrs. E. Shaw |
| 1929 | Miss Shackles | 1973 | Mrs. N. R. Green |
| 1930 | Mrs. Stanley Earle | 1974 | Mrs. T. C. Doughty |
| 1931 | Mrs. Frost | 1975 | Mrs. R. P. Wreathall |
| 1932 | Mrs. T. Wells | 1976 | Miss J. Clappison |
| 1933 | Mrs. A. E. Craft | 1977 | Miss C. M. Waddell |
| 1934 | Mrs. N. Johnson | 1978 | Mrs. G. J. F. Alexander |
| 1935 | Mrs. A. W. Todd | 1979 | Mrs. J. R. Binnington |
| 1936 | Mrs. Proctor | 1980 | Mrs. R. J. Wood |
| 1937 | Miss M. Kemp | 1981 | Mrs. S. L. Wright |
| 1938 | Mrs. Proctor | 1982 | Mrs. R. Reynolds |
| 1939 | Miss F. Booth | 1983 | Mrs. A. A. Clarke |
| 1946 | Mrs. Proctor | 1984 | Mrs. D. W. Kirby |
| 1947 | Mrs. Proctor | 1985 | Mrs. J. Waine |
| 1948 | Mrs. Proctor | 1986 | Mrs. W. Armstrong |
| 1949 | Mrs. Proctor | 1987 | Mrs. P. B. Metcalfe |
| 1950 | Mrs. M. Kemp | 1988 | Mrs. S. Charter |
| 1951 | Mrs. Whitehead | 1989 | Mrs. W. R. Skern |
| 1952 | Mrs. Wells | 1990 | Mrs. M. E. Smith |
| 1953 | Mrs. Kirkus | 1991 | Mrs. A. Hardy |
| 1954 | Mrs. Earle | 1992 | Mrs. S. Stead |
| 1955 | Mrs. Bastow | 1993 | Mrs. P. Kirton |
| 1956 | Mrs. Green | 1994 | Mrs. A. C. Blood |
| 1957 | Mrs. H. S. Biggs | 1995 | Mrs. R. H. Leonard |
| 1958 | Mrs. E. L. Biggs | 1996 | Mrs. M. R. Smith |
| 1959 | Mrs. S. G. French | 1997 | Mrs. J. L. Muirhead |
| 1960 | Mrs. T. N. Stephenson | | |
| 1961 | Mrs. W. J. Ingram | | |

## Appendix 5

### Junior Captains

| | | | | |
|---|---|---|---|---|
| 1978 | M. Binnington | | 1988 | R. Close |
| 1979 | J. White | | 1989 | R. Muschamp |
| 1980 | D. Oliver | | 1990 | R. Muschamp |
| 1981 | K. Wright | | 1991 | P. Latus |
| 1982 | D. Haymes | | 1992 | J. Hart |
| 1983 | C. Wilson | | 1993 | J. Lewis |
| 1984 | P. Binnington | | 1995 | P. Turner |
| 1985 | N. Haymes | | 1996 | R. Varley |
| 1986 | G. Williams | | 1997 | P. Robson |
| 1987 | M. Carmichael | | | |

# Appendix 6
## Honorary Life Members

Mr. A. F. H. Lax
Mr. H. M. Lumley
Mr. J. A. Stout
Mr. T. J. Thirsk
Mr. G. S. Wade
Mr. S. Stenhouse
Mr. E. L. Biggs
Mrs. G. Earle
Mrs. M. Toogood
Mr. D. Ferraby
Mr. I. D. McIntyre
Mr. D. P. Shackles

Mr. A. Renshaw
Mr. R. M. Roach
Mr. R. S. F. Brown
Mr. T. Tomlinson
Mr. P. T. Wright
M,r. N. P. Seaton
Mr. M. Hesk
Mrs. J. L. Major
Mrs. M. Kirkus
Mr. B. Falkingham
Mr. C. H. Lax

# Appendix 7
## Gentlemen Members in 1997

| Name | Joined H.G.C. | Name | Joined H.G.C. |
|---|---|---|---|
| Lax, Mr. C. H. | 26. 1.37 | Kirby, Mr. D. W. | 5. 2.65 |
| Marson, Mr. D. W. | 19. 4.48 | Dunn, Mr. T. D. | 5. 5.65 |
| Hanger, Mr. E. | 19. 6.50 | Hampton, Mr. F. J. | 7. 5.66 |
| Blenkin, Mr. H. H. | 23.10.50 | Armstrong, Mr. W. | 11. 6.66 |
| Hornby, Mr. D. A. | 19. 2.51 | Blackburn, Mr. E. | 27. 7.66 |
| Kidd, Mr. J. V. | 9. 8.51 | Mortimer, Mr. A. E. | 27. 7.66 |
| Bolton, Mr. B. | 16. 3.53 | Smith, Mr. A. E. | 27. 7.66 |
| Cawkill, Mr. P. S. | 21. 6.55 | Smith, Mr. C. T. | 27. 7.66 |
| Sargent, Mr. A. H. | 3. 9.57 | Dunn, Mr. C. S. | 31. 1.67 |
| Tomlinson, Mr. H. D. | 15. 4.58 | Geddes, Mr. T. J. | 31. 1.67 |
| Taylor, Mr. J. L. | 15. 5.58 | Anderson, Mr. J. W. | 1. 2.67 |
| Davern, Rev. M. | 27. 1.59 | Ball, Mr. D. | 30. 6.67 |
| Taylor, Mr. K. C. | 24. 2.59 | Blacker, Mr. D. A. | 27 .2.68 |
| Dibnah, Mr. J. R. | 19. 1.60 | Bird, Mr. P. A. | 30. 4.68 |
| Coates, Mr. G. B. | 16. 8.60 | Baxter, Mr. R. C. | 25. 6.68 |
| Binnington, Mr. J. R. | 16. 5.61 | Woodmansey, Mr. K. | 25. 6.68 |
| Holmes, Mr. R. | 25. 7.61 | Jobey, Mr. J. R. | 6. 8.68 |
| Hesk, Mr. M. | 21.10.61 | Brown, Mr. W. | 24. 9.68 |
| Knott, Mr. F. W. | 12. 1.62 | Branton, Mr. W. | 1. 1.69 |
| Schofield, Mr. J. D. | 14. 6.62 | Hunter, Mr. M. | 7. 1.69 |
| Smith, Mr. P. | 8. 4.63 | Ellis, Mr. P. M. | 29. 4.69 |
| Burn, Mr. H. A. | 10. 4.63 | Griffiths, Mr. M. R. | 29. 4.69 |
| Metcalfe, Mr. C. W. | 4. 5.63 | Taylor, Mr. G. N. | 29. 4.69 |
| Bullivent, Mr. H. | 10. 6.63 | Train, Mr. E. S. | 29. 4.69 |
| Gregg, Mr. A. | 19. 6.63 | Richardson, Mr. G. | 20. 5.69 |
| Atkins, Mr. P. W. | 26. 6.63 | Roberts, Mr. C. S. | 24. 6.69 |
| Yonge, Mr. G. C. | 21. 9.63 | Stark, Mr. A. M. | 24. 6.69 |
| Yonge, Mr. J. D. | 21. 9.63 | Jones, Mr. T. | 26. 6.69 |
| Crawford, Mr. P. | 4.11.63 | Allen, Mr. D. | 29. 7.69 |
| Skern, Mr. W. R. | 1.12.63 | Jones, Mr. D. A. | 29. 7.69 |
| Deacon, Dr. D. F. C. | 5.12.63 | Moore, Mr. G. S. | 29. 7.69 |
| Stead, Mr. D. | 1. 1.64 | Spriggs, Mr. R. G. | 29. 7.69 |
| Roberts, Mr. S. | 16. 6.64 | Copley, Mr. D. | 26. 8.69 |
| Charter, Mr. Richard | 14.11.64 | Bennett, Mr. J. H. | 30.12.69 |
| Boyd, Mr. R. W. | 1.12.64 | Brown, Mr. Malcolm | 30.12.69 |
| Bird, Mr. F. D. | 2. 2.65 | Foster, Mr. W. K. | 30.12.69 |

| Name | Joined H.G.C. | Name | Joined H.G.C. |
|---|---|---|---|
| Arnott, Mr. A. | 28. 4.70 | Garton, Mr. P. M. | 22. 5.75 |
| Davies, Mr. M. L. | 30. 6.70 | L'Anson, Mr. R. | 22. 5.75 |
| Palmer, Mr. H. C. | 28. 7.70 | Allen, Mr. R. H. | 8. 7.75 |
| Dunn, Mr. R. L. | 29. 9.70 | Jackson, Mr. P. | 9. 7.75 |
| Moore, Mr. M. E. G. | 29.12.70 | Hammersley, Mr. M. F. | 10. 7.75 |
| Hemingway, Mr. A. C. | 30. 3.71 | Croft, Mr. E. A. | 11. 7.75 |
| Read, Mr. P. | 29.10.71 | Scott, Mr. J. | 11. 8.75 |
| Slaven, Mr. P. F. | 19.12.71 | Ayres, Mr. Alan | 27. 1.76 |
| Mewburn, Mr. J. H. | 28.12.71 | Broxham, Mr. N. H. | 27. 1.76 |
| Blades, Mr. E. C. | 26. 1.72 | Grantham, Mr. B. | 23. 2.76 |
| Palin, Mr. F. A. | 1. 2.72 | Dean, Mr. F. H. | 1. 3.76 |
| Hodgson, Mr. D. V. | 21. 3.72 | Inman, Mr. C. R. | 1. 3.76 |
| Dibnah, Mr. A. L. | 25. 4.72 | Robinson, Mr. E. V. | 1. 3.76 |
| Gorbutt, Mr. M. | 15. 5.72 | Foord, Mr. N. J. | 2. 3.76 |
| Waite, Mr. J. | 1. 6.72 | Arnold, Mr. C. B. | 4. 3.76 |
| Railton, Mr. R. N. | 5. 6.72 | Calverley, Mr. A. | 8. 3.76 |
| Clarke, Mr. D. H. | 10. 7.72 | Quibell, Mr. J. G. W. | 8. 3.76 |
| Parry, Mr. K. | 26. 9.72 | Ellenton, Mr. L. H. | 3. 5.76 |
| Ellarby, Mr. C. L. | 16. 1.73 | Wright, Mr. R. G. | 24. 5.76 |
| Stephenson, Mr. W. G. | 30. 1.73 | Horsfield, Mr. M. | 14. 9.76 |
| Gell, Mr. G. | 14. 2.73 | Taylor, Mr. John D. | 14. 9.76 |
| Sharples, Mr. E. J. | 31. 5.73 | Appleton, Mr. G. | 13.12.76 |
| Wright, Mr. S. L. | 8. 6.73 | Varley, Mr. C. | 6. 5.77 |
| Butler, Mr. A. H. | 10. 7.73 | Varley, Mr. M. J. F. | 6. 5.77 |
| Muir, Mr. A. J. | 22.10.73 | Varley, Mr. T. C. | 6. 5.77 |
| Scott, Mr. J. A. | 21. 1.74 | Bielby, Mr. C. C. | 10. 5.77 |
| Waterson, Mr. H. A. | 23. 1.74 | Walker, Mr. J. F. | 18. 7.77 |
| Nelson, Mr. A. P. | 25. 2.74 | Clarke, Mr. A. A. | 16. 1.78 |
| Medcalfe, Mr. E. H. | 4. 3.74 | Jackson, Mr. M. W. | 10. 2.78 |
| Bannister, Mr. P. | 13. 5.74 | Taylor, Mr. John Royston | 15. 2.78 |
| Richards, Mr. D. | 13. 5.74 | Ralph, Mr. A. | 30. 3.78 |
| Dawson, Mr. D. A. | 20. 5.74 | Dale, Mr. S. | 12. 6.78 |
| Norton, Mr. F. A. | 9. 7.74 | Ducker, Mr. R. | 16. 6.78 |
| Moore, Mr. C. R. | 13.10.74 | Atkin, Mr. P. D. | 17. 7.78 |
| Moran, Mr. E. | 24.10.74 | Belcher, Mr. M. W. | 17. 7.78 |
| Longley, Mr. J. V. | 6. 1.75 | Scott, Mr. R. | 29. 1.79 |
| Bielby, Mr. R. H. | 28. 2.75 | Dickinson, Mr. R. | 4. 4.79 |
| Reynolds, Mr. R. | 14. 4.75 | Clarke, Mr. M. M. | 9. 4.79 |
| Smith, Mr. D. J. | 14. 4.75 | Farley, Mr. B. | 9. 4.79 |
| Dale, Mr. G. I. E. | 28. 4.75 | Nippress, Mr. B. | 11. 6.79 |
| Hammersley. Mr. J. F. | 21. 5.75 | Holloway, Mr. R. L. | 10. 9.79 |
| Cook, Mr. Ron | 22. 5.75 | Tuton, Mr. R. | 12. 9.79 |

| Name | Joined H.G.C. | Name | Joined H.G.C. |
|------|---------------|------|---------------|
| Close, Mr. T. | 26.11.79 | Waite, Mr. C. J. | 21.11.83 |
| McGlone, Mr. P. B. | 7.12.79 | Matthews, Mr. . R. | 12.12.83 |
| Varley, Mr. M. R. | 4. 2.80 | Williamson, Mr. M. J. | 12.12.83 |
| Varley, Mr. J. S. | 25. 2.80 | Maharry, Mr. P. W. | 8. 2.84 |
| Foord, Mr. A. | 15. 4.80 | Nightingale, Mr. W. | 8. 2.84 |
| Hobson, Mr. P. L. | 19. 5.80 | Gibbins, Mr. R. E. | 13. 2.84 |
| Purshouse, Mr. L. D. | 28. 6.80 | Silverwood, Mr. R. D. | 6. 3.84 |
| Jordan, Mr. F. D. | 18. 8.80 | Borrill, Mr. D. J. | 9. 3.84 |
| Wrigglesworth, Mr. A. | 29. 8.80 | Lewis, Mr. I. H. | 26. 4.84 |
| Dickins, Mr. J. M. | 3. 2.81 | Cook, Mr. R. | 30. 4.84 |
| Ellerby, Mr. A. | 3. 2.81 | Hodgson, Mr. J. S. | 23. 5.84 |
| Laughton, Mr. D. | 3. 2.81 | Smith, Mr. D. | 2. 7.84 |
| McIntosh, Mr. I. D. | 3. 2.81 | Revell, Mr. J. F. | 10. 9.84 |
| Vere, Mr. B. A. | 18. 5.81 | Ward, Mr. J. B. | 31.10.84 |
| Drinkall, Mr. P. G. | 1. 6.81 | Meadley, Mr. J. R. | 19.11.84 |
| Winn, Mr. S. | 12. 6.81 | Todd, Mr. M. | 19.11.84 |
| Leonard, Mr. G. T. | 22. 7.81 | Anderson, Mr. D. M. | 8. 1.85 |
| Jordan, Mr. S. H. | 10. 8.81 | Williams, Mr. T. A. | 8. 1.85 |
| Ingram, Mr. P. F. A. | 26.10.81 | Williamson, Mr. W. S. | 8. 1.85 |
| Smith, Mr. V. | 19.11.81 | Peasgood, Mr. B. | 29. 1.85 |
| Blood, Mr. R. J. | 18. 1.82 | Jewitt, Mr. K. | 30. 4.85 |
| Etherington, Mr. T. A. | 4. 2.82 | Frith, Mr. P. W. | 2. 7.85 |
| Brown, Mr. A. | 5. 2.82 | Jefferson, Mr. A. | 2. 7.85 |
| Bickenson, Mr. J. E. | 22. 2.82 | Smallwood, Mr. J. | 2. 7.85 |
| Johnson, Mr. H. | 22. 2.82 | Goodwin, Mr. G. E. | 15. 7.85 |
| Sheppard, Mr. J. A. | 24. 2.82 | Gorton, Mr. K. | 12. 8.85 |
| Brooke, Mr. M. E. | 8. 3.82 | Robinson, Mr. A. D. | 12. 8.85 |
| Williams, Mr. G. | 10. 5.82 | Brown, Mr. P. A. | 16.12.85 |
| Hall, Colonel O. T. | 14. 6.82 | Cooper, Mr. S. | 6. 1.86 |
| Prout, Mr. I. G. | 8.12.82 | Johnson, Mr. A. | 8. 1.86 |
| Hornby, Mr. D. G. | 15. 1.83 | Barron, Mr. A. J. | 14. 1.86 |
| Cutts, Mr. T. | 24. 1.83 | Anderson, Mr. S. J. | 10. 2.86 |
| Mason, Mr. G. A. | 1. 2.83 | Hall, Mr. F. J. | 25. 2.86 |
| Thacker, Mr. G. A. | 28. 3.83 | Jordison, Mr. J. R. | 15. 5.86 |
| Barton, Mr. S. R. | 11. 4.83 | Cooke, Mr. J. D. | 17. 7.86 |
| Hardy, Mr. J. | 18. 4.83 | Latus, Mr. R. | 11. 8.86 |
| Nettleton, Mr. G. | 26. 4.83 | Jennings, Mr. A. J. | 12. 8.86 |
| Anderson, Mr. D. H. | 5. 8.83 | Harness, Mr. E. S. | 21. 8.86 |
| Atkin, Mr. C. H. | 21. 8.83 | Taylor, Mr. D. P. | 21. 8.86 |
| Coates, Mr. P. L. | 21. 8.83 | Curtis, Mr. S. J. | 9. 9.86 |
| Davy, Mr. C. | 26. 9.83 | Elliott, Mr. H. R. | 26. 9.86 |
| Holdsworth, Mr. D. M. | 21.10.83 | Raines, Mr. P. M. | 17.11.86 |

| Name | Joined H.G.C. | Name | Joined H.G.C. |
|---|---|---|---|
| Robinson, Mr. A. P. | 17.11.86 | Lydiat, Mr. J. | 5.11.88 |
| Curtis, Mr. J. W. P. | 18.11.86 | Barnsley, Mr. A. C. | 1. 1.89 |
| Fitchett, Mr. L. | 9.12.86 | Bennett, Mr. John E. | 1. 1.89 |
| Lockwood, Mr. B. | 9.12.86 | Clappison, Mr. A. M. | 1. 1.89 |
| Broadbent, Mr. W. | 1. 1.87 | Crossland, Mr. Max C. | 1. 1.89 |
| Kirton, Mr. B. W. | 1. 1.87 | Eastwood, Mr. P. | 1. 1.89 |
| Baker, Mr. A. E. | 1. 4.87 | Evans, Mr. Colin J. | 1. 1.89 |
| Bond, Mr. K. D. | 1. 4.87 | Helm, Mr. Paul | 1. 1.89 |
| Kitchen, Mr. B. A. | 1. 4.87 | Johnson, Mr. W. J. | 1. 1.89 |
| Bibby, Mr. D. S. JK. | 6. 4.87 | Merritt, Mr. Kenneth | 1. 1.89 |
| Ingram, Mr. D. | 1. 5.87 | Milner, Mr. N. S. | 1. 1.89 |
| Matson, Mr. J. | 1. 5.87 | Porter, Mr. J. D. | 1. 1.89 |
| Evans, Mr. B. | 1. 7.87 | Prince, Mr. J. W. | 1. 1.89 |
| Goforth, Mr. J. W. | 18. 8.87 | Raw, Mr. C. R. | 1. 1.89 |
| Sheppard, Mr. C. P. | 1. 9.87 | Robinson, Mr. P. | 1. 1.89 |
| Curtis, Mr. D. G. W. | 16. 9.87 | Scrivens, Mr. William C. | 1. 1.89 |
| Page, Mr. J. B. | 16. 9.87 | Whitton, Mr. D. J. | 1. 1.89 |
| Hall, Mr. S. | 27.10.87 | Windass, Mr. Roy J. | 1. 1.89 |
| Dudill, Mr. P. | 1. 1.88 | Gallagher, Rev. Francis G | 1. 4.89 |
| Lloyd, Mr. D. G. | 1. 1.88 | Kaye, Mr. David | 1. 4.89 |
| Owen, Mr. C. M. | 1. 1.88 | Clappison, Mr. T. I. | 1. 5.89 |
| Smith, Mr. G. | 1. 1.88 | Prout, Mr. Malcolm L. | 1. 5.89 |
| Egan, Rev. P. | 26. 1.88 | Muirhead, Mr. M. R. | 1. 6.89 |
| Walker, Mr. R. P. | 11. 2.88 | Jackson, Mr. P. G. | 1. 7.89 |
| Colley, Mr. N. T. | 3. 3.88 | Needham, Mr. J. W. | 1. 7.89 |
| Wilkinson, Mr. C. | 23. 3.88 | Wilson, Mr. P. | 1. 7.89 |
| Johnson, Mr. P. R. | 12. 4.88 | Scaife, Mr. D. | 27. 7.89 |
| Dinning, Mr. I. R. | 24. 5.88 | Wright, Mr. A. | 1.11.89 |
| Magee, Mr. J. | 1. 6.88 | Appleby, Mr. G. R. | 1.12.89 |
| Pickering, Mr. P. | 1. 6.88 | Walshaw, Mr. P. | 1.12.89 |
| Gill, Rev. T. | 14. 7.88 | Beighton, Mr. J. | 22. 3.90 |
| Gray, Mr. M. A. | 1. 8.88 | Blake, Mr. J. M. | 22. 3.90 |
| Thompson, Mr. A. J. | 2. 8.88 | Burdon, Mr. C. D. | 22. 3.90 |
| Cook, Mr. N. | 16. 8.88 | Jackson, Mr. R. C. | 22. 3.90 |
| Jordan, Mr. N. J. | 16. 8.88 | Marson, Mr. A. D. | 22. 3.90 |
| Wilkinson, Mr. S. J. | 26. 8.88 | Prescott, Mr. A. | 22. 3.90 |
| Linter, Mr. D. | 1. 9.88 | Skow, Mr. B. | 22. 3.90 |
| Atkins, Mr. G. B. | 13. 9.88 | Townhill, Mr. H. W. | 22. 3.90 |
| Clegg, Mr. A. | 13. 9.88 | Hart, Mr. J. P. | 1. 7.90 |
| Lockwood, Mr. A. | 13. 9.88 | Hart, Mr. P. B. | 1. 7.90 |
| Wilkinson, Mr. S. | 1.10.88 | Fewson, Mr. C. W. | 19. 7.90 |
| Rhodes, Mr. B. | 8.10.88 | Hodgson, Mr. P. | 19. 7.90 |

| Name | Joined H.G.C. | Name | Joined H.G.C. |
|------|------|------|------|
| Humphrey, Mr. J. F. | 19. 7.90 | Saunders, Mr. M. C. | 17. 2.92 |
| Prescott, Mr. D. M. | 19. 7.90 | Clayton, Mr. J. E. | 21. 2.92 |
| Whitchurch, Mr. J. | 19. 7.90 | White, Rev. M. | 1. 3.92 |
| Cappleman, Mr. O. L. | 10. 8.90 | Stott, Mr. M. D. | 31. 7.92 |
| Keogh, Rev. M. | 22.10.90 | Fletcher, Mr. K. M. | 1. 8.92 |
| Gillard, Mr. I. S. | 1. 1.91 | Bowling, Mr. S. F. | 1. 9.92 |
| Smith, Mr. J. D. | 1. 1.91 | Browne, Mr. R. A. | 1. 9.92 |
| Smith, Mr. M. A. | 1. 1.91 | Huxley, Mr. D. W. | 1. 9.92 |
| Alexander, Mr. R. | 1. 3.91 | Peart, Mr. M. | 1. 9.92 |
| Allon, Mr. D. | 1. 3.91 | Towse, Mr. S. | 1. 9.92 |
| Atkinson, Mr. G. A. | 1. 3.91 | Cunliffe, Mr. R. J. D. | 3. 9.92 |
| Blackburn, Mr. T. | 1. 3.91 | Thornton, Mr. P. | 8. 9.92 |
| Broady, Mr. T. | 1. 3.91 | Parker, Mr. M. G. | 26. 2.93 |
| Brogan, Mr. I. W. | 1. 3.91 | Botham, Mr. N. | 1. 3.93 |
| Broughton, Mr. F. | 1. 3.91 | Bray, Mr. K. R. | 1. 3.93 |
| Draper, Mr. C. D. | 1. 3.91 | Butcher, Mr. G. R. | 1. 3.93 |
| Dunford, Mr. R. H. | 1. 3.91 | Coates, Mr. A. | 1. 3.93 |
| Edmondson, Mr. J. S. | 1. 3.91 | Collingwood, Mr. E. E. | 1. 3.93 |
| Egerton, Mr. J. | 1. 3.91 | Jellyman, Mr. R. H. | 1. 3.93 |
| Giles, Mr. J. G. | 1. 3.91 | Marshall, Mr. P. J. T. | 1. 3.93 |
| Gilroy, Mr. M. A. | 1. 3.91 | Millar, Mr. S. | 1. 3.93 |
| Grazier, Mr. J. V. | 1. 3.91 | Playfoot, Mr. Q. R. | 1. 3.93 |
| Lissimore, MT. G. T. | 1. 3.91 | Procter, Mr. H. G. | 1. 3.93 |
| Moore, Mr. D. T. | 1. 3.91 | Robinson, Mr. S. | 1. 3.93 |
| Nippress, Mr. P. | 1. 3.91 | Samuel, Mr. I. N. | 1. 3.93 |
| Prothero, Mr. P. C. | 1. 3.91 | Turner, Mr. B. B. | 1. 3.93 |
| Scott, Mr. P. | 1. 3.91 | Wilkinson, Dr. M. | 1. 3.93 |
| Semple, Mr. H. | 1. 3.91 | Todd, Mr. P. | 1. 6.93 |
| Sheedy, Mr. P. K. | 1. 3.91 | Crossman, Mr. J. R. | 1. 7.93 |
| Stott, Mr. R. A. | 1. 3.91 | Ballington, Mr. J. L. | 1. 4.94 |
| Telford, Mr. P. D. | 1. 3.91 | Boyd, Dr. P. A. | 1. 4.94 |
| Stead, Mr. I. | 1. 4.91 | Hall, Mr. J. J. | 1. 4.94 |
| Acklam, Mr. P. | 30. 7.91 | Hooton, Mr. R. | 1. 4.94 |
| Young, Mr. C. C. | 1.12.91 | Laycock, Mr. M. | 1. 4.94 |
| Lockwood, Mr. P. | 10. 2.92 | McKie, Mr. C. R. | 1. 4.94 |
| Usher, Mr. D. R. | 10. 2.92 | Morris, Mr. S. | 1. 4.94 |
| Bridges, Mr. P. J. | 14. 2.92 | Pittaway, Mr. M. S. | 1. 4.94 |
| Cansdale, Mr. N. | 14. 2.92 | Richardson, Mr. R. | 1. 4.94 |
| Little, Mr. C. E. | 14. 2.92 | Scamans, Mr. F. | 1. 4.94 |
| Massey, Mr. B. | 14. 2.92 | Sparkes, Mr. G. | 1. 4.94 |
| Rogerson, Mr. M. D. | 14. 2.92 | Stavely, Mr. A. E. | 1. 4.94 |
| Strachan, Mr. M. D. | 14. 2.92 | Stevenson, Mr. D. | 1. 4.94 |

| Name | Joined H.G.C. | Name | Joined H.G.C. |
|---|---|---|---|
| Vahey, Mr. M. A. | 1. 4.94 | Myers, Mr. J. R. W. | 1. 4.96 |
| Williams, Mr. K. | 1. 4.94 | Nolan, Mr. M. | 1. 4.96 |
| Woodall, Mr. M. J. | 1. 4.94 | Pettman, Prof. B. O. | 1. 4.96 |
| Wray, Mr. R. E. | 1. 4.94 | Slingsby, Mr. P. D. | 1. 4.96 |
| Hawkins, Mr. S. R. | 14.11.94 | Walby, Mr. L. D. | 1. 4.96 |
| Northgraves, Mr. A. P. | 14.11.94 | Thompson, Mr. B. C. | 14. 5.96 |
| Rhodes, Mr. K. | 14.11.94 | Lamb, Mr. M. | 1. 8.96 |
| Smith, Mr. A. | 14.11.94 | Bell, Mr. W. R. | 1.11.96 |
| Wood, Mr. B. A. C. | 14.11.94 | Francis, Mr. J. | 13.11.96 |
| Northgraves, Mr. J. P. | 21.11.94 | Osbourne, Mr. D. J. | 13.11.96 |
| Close, Mr. B. R. | 1. 1.95 | Robson, Mr. D. | 13.11.96 |
| Hine, Mr. C. | 13. 1.95 | Barber, Mr. P. | 18.11.96 |
| Richardson, Mr. M. C. | 2. 3.95 | Charles, Mr. G. E. | 20.11.96 |
| Coates, Mr. P. A. | 10. 4.95 | Clappison, Mr. N. E. | 20.11.96 |
| Fisk, Mr. G. A. | 10. 4.95 | Conman, Mr. S. P. | 20.11.96 |
| Holroyd, Mr. R. L. | 10. 4.95 | Conner, Mr. G. D. | 20.11.96 |
| Moulds, Mr. C. S. | 10. 4.95 | Froud, Mr. J. H. | 20.11.96 |
| Roberts, Mr. E. J. | 10. 4.95 | Hindle, Mr. M. G. | 20.11.96 |
| Rotherham, Mr. P. | 10. 4.95 | Kirby, Mr. T. | 20.11.96 |
| Setterfield, Mr. N. M. | 10. 4.95 | Lockey, Mr. K. | 20.11.96 |
| Stead, Mr. R. | 10. 4.95 | Marshall, Mr. K. L. | 20.11.96 |
| Wills, Mr. P. D. | 10. 4.95 | Midgley, Mr. A. | 20.11.96 |
| Robinson, Mr. R. | 16. 6.95 | Rhodes, Mr. D. | 20.11.96 |
| Cowie, Mr. S. G. | 1. 8.95 | Robinson, Mr. P. M. | 20.11.96 |
| Fitchett, Mr. A. F. | 1. 8.95 | Sienko, Mr. M. | 20.11.96 |
| Osborne, Mr. J. M. | 1. 8.95 | Stone, Mr. T. | 20.11.96 |
| Wray, Mr. S. P. | 1. 8.95 | Train, Mr. M. | 20.11.96 |
| O'Donnell, Rev. S. | 18.12.95 | Turner, Mr. D. J. | 20.11.96 |
| Hayes, Mr. B. J. | 20.12.95 | Wood, Mr. Robert J. | 20.11.96 |
| Jarvis, Mr. I. F. | 20.12.95 | Wray, Mr. M. J. | 20.11.96 |
| Jewitt, Mr. A. K. | 20.12.95 | Woodall, Mr. S. W. | |
| Platten, Mr. D. A. | 20.12.95 | Railton, Mr. A. R. | 6. 5.97 |
| Reeve, Mr. J. | 20.12.95 | Osbourne, Mr. R. | 6. 5.97 |
| Wood, Mr. S. M. | 20.12.95 | Robson, Mr. D. | 6. 5.97 |
| Cordock, Mr. J. | 4. 1.96 | Staveley, Mr. P. A. | 6. 5.97 |
| Bell, Mr. M. A. | 20. 3.96 | Pearson, Mr. A. | 6. 5.97 |
| Bucknall, Mr. G. P. | 1. 4.96 | Lison, Mr. J. M. | 6. 5.97 |
| Claughton, Mr. J. A. H. | 1. 4.96 | Wilson, Mr. D. S. | 6. 5.97 |
| Davis, Mr. R. M. | 1. 4.96 | Banks, Mr. P. A. | 6. 5.97 |
| Jackson, Mr. A. R. | 1. 4.96 | Wilson, Mr. C. J. | 6. 5.97 |
| Johnston, Mr. R. M. | 1. 4.96 | Turner, Mr. D. | 6. 5.97 |
| Lilley, B. | 1. 4.96 | Swann, Mr. K. | 6. 5.97 |
| | | Aherne, Mr. M. | 6. 5.97 |

## Appendix 8
### Lady Members in 1997

| Name | Joined H.G.C. | Name | Joined H.G.C. |
|------|------|------|------|
| Biggs, Mrs. H. S. | 9. 6.47 | Roach, Miss J. G. | 20. 1.76 |
| Burn, Mrs. B. | 16. 3.53 | Clarke, Mrs. K. J. | 16. 1.78 |
| Dyson, Mrs. Margaret | 18. 1.54 | Blacker, Mrs. W. B. | 28. 3.78 |
| Hurn, Mrs. D. K. | 20.12.55 | Marson, Mrs. E. J. | 4. 9.78 |
| Major, Mrs. M. J. | 18. 6.56 | Atkins, Mrs. J. | 26. 9.78 |
| Smith, Mrs. L. | 18. 2.58 | Atkin, Mrs. R. | 9. 1.79 |
| Bullivant, Mrs. C. | 21. 4.59 | Moore, Mrs. M. | 19. 1.80 |
| Taylor, Mrs. M. | 16.10.59 | Stead, Mrs. S. | 13. 5.80 |
| Wood, Mrs. C. | 21. 6.60 | Jordan, Mrs. S. A. | 10. 8.81 |
| Metcalfe, Mrs. I. W. | 11. 2.63 | Smith, Mrs. M. R. | 18.11.81 |
| Binnington, Mrs. P. J. | 18. 4.63 | Smith, Mrs. M. E. | 15.11.82 |
| Skern, Mrs. B. C. | 4.12.63 | Grantham, Mrs. E. C. | 22. 2.83 |
| Iveson, Mrs. L. | 8. 1.65 | Hardy, Mrs. A. | 18. 4.83 |
| Fluck, Mrs. P. M. | 9. 1.65 | Lewis, Mrs. M. C. | 31.10.83 |
| Kirby, Mrs. M. R. | 17. 3.65 | Moran, Mrs. Elizabeth | 2. 2.84 |
| Bird, Mrs. J. V. | 26. 4.66 | Revell, Mrs. J. M. | 10. 9.84 |
| Wreathall, Mrs. S. L. | 26. 4.66 | Webster, Mrs. M. | 12. 9.84 |
| Donkin, Mrs. D. | 8. 9.66 | Grant, Mrs. M. M. | 26.10.84 |
| Leonard, Mrs. S. | 25.10.66 | Meadley, Mrs. M. | 19.11.84 |
| Armstrong, Mrs. E. P. | 29.11.66 | Wrigglesworth, Mrs. E. E. | 8. 1.85 |
| Clappison, Miss J. | 20. 5.69 | Egerton, Mrs. S. E. | 3. 4.85 |
| Smith, Mrs. B. I. | 20. 5.69 | Gorton, Mrs. C. L. | 12. 8.85 |
| Jackson, Mrs. M. C. | 4. 6.69 | Robinson, Mrs. D. | 12. 8.85 |
| Stark, Mrs. C. M. | 24. 6.69 | Robinson, Mrs. S. M. | 7. 9.85 |
| Smith, Mrs. E. M. | 29. 7.69 | Moore, Mrs. A. | 29. 1.86 |
| Charter, Mrs. S. | 26. 8.69 | Johnson, Mrs. E. | 14. 5.86 |
| Foster, Mrs. B. I. | 30.12.69 | Mewburn, Mrs. D. M. | 17.11.86 |
| Anderson, Mrs. A. J. | 29.12.70 | Blood, Mrs. A. C. | 11.12.86 |
| Waine, Mrs. J. | 30. 5.72 | Kirton, Mrs. P. A. | 1. 1.87 |
| Thompson, Mrs. J. | 28. 5.74 | Appleton, Mrs. J. | 11. 2.87 |
| Wright, Mrs. J. E. | 30. 7.74 | Baker, Mrs. M. E. | 1. 4.87 |
| Sharples, Mrs. S. S. | 21. 4.75 | Anderson, Mrs. A. | 1. 1.88 |
| Hammersley, Mrs. P. S. | 21. 5.75 | Samuel, Mrs. K. D. | 22. 1.88 |
| Dalby, Mrs. P. J. | 20.10.75 | Clarke, Mrs. C. | 12. 5.88 |
| Reynolds, Mrs. P. | 20.10.75 | Woodall, Mrs. J. | 16. 5.88 |
| Richardson, Mrs. A. E. | 19. 1.76 | Dinning, Mrs. M. | 1. 6.88 |

| Name | Joined H.G.C. | Name | Joined H.G.C. |
|---|---|---|---|
| Gill, Mrs. M. | 1. 8.88 | Young, Mrs. J. | 19. 5.92 |
| Clappison, Mrs. P. M. | 2. 8.88 | Jackson, Mrs. J. | 25. 1.93 |
| Merritt, Mrs. A. | 2. 8.88 | Yonge, Mrs. E. C. | 25. 1.93 |
| McCaughey, | | Hodgson, Mrs. V. C. | 1. 3.93 |
| Mrs. Doreen G. | 1. 1.89 | Jefferson, Mrs. S. | 1. 3.93 |
| Wilson, Mrs. Judith O. | 1. 1.89 | Caley, Mrs. C. | 19. 3.93 |
| Hall, Mrs. E. | 1. 2.89 | Bond, Mrs. L. | 28. 3.94 |
| Porter, Mrs. L. | 1. 2.89 | Richardson, Mrs. M. A. | 28. 3.94 |
| Thornton, Mrs. Judith | 1. 5.89 | Vierucci, Mrs. J. | 28. 3.94 |
| Muirhead, Mrs. J. Louise | 1. 6.89 | Ayres, Mrs. P. A. | 1. 4.94 |
| Barron, Mrs. P. E. | 1. 7.89 | Coates, Mrs. A. V. | 1. 4.94 |
| Scaife, Mrs. P. M. | 1. 7.90 | Ballington, Mrs. E. A. | 2. 2.95 |
| Grazier, Mrs. J. | 1. 3.91 | Bell, Mrs. F. M. | 2. 2.95 |
| Rowbottom, Mrs. C. M. | 1. 4.91 | Gittus, Mrs. P. | 21. 8.95 |
| Clarke, Mrs. S. | 25. 2.92 | Pettman, Mrs. M. | 26. 2.96 |
| Andrews, Miss J. | 6. 3.92 | Grantham, Mrs. S. | 1. 4.96 |
| Clappison, Mrs. A. | 19. 5.92 | | |

## Appendix 9
### Junior Student Members in 1997

| Name | Joined H.G.C. | Name | Joined H.G.C. |
|---|---|---|---|
| Muir, Mr. A. J. | 22.10.73 | Thompson, Mr. A. J. | 2. 8.88 |
| Williams, Mr. G. | 10. 5.82 | Humphrey, Mr. J. F. | 19. 7.90 |
| Anderson, Mr. S. J. | 10. 2.86 | Whitchurch, Mr. J. | 19. 7.90 |
| Goforth, Mr. J. W. | 18. 8.87 | Cappleman, Mr. O. L. | 10. 8.90 |
| Hall, Mr. S. | 27.10.87 | Gillard, Mr. I. S. | 1. 1.91 |
| Palmer, Miss C. M. | 11. 2.88 | Stott, Mr. M. D. | 31. 7.92 |
| Walker, Mr. R. P. | 11. 2.88 | Robinson, Mr. R. | 16. 6.95 |
| Wrigglesworth, Miss K. | 22. 3.88 | | |

# Appendix 10
## Junior Members in 1997

| Name | Joined H.G.C. | Name | Joined H.G.C. |
|---|---|---|---|
| Laughton, Mr. C. | 26. 3.88 | Varley, Mr. R. J. | 1. 1.94 |
| Peasgood, Mr. M. R. | 1. 8.90 | Sharples, Mr. J. J. | 13. 1.94 |
| Close, Miss J. | 10. 8.90 | Setterfield, Mr. S. | 28. 3.94 |
| Palmer, Mr. D. J. | 10. 8.90 | Taylor, Mr. T. W. J. | 1. 4.94 |
| Hart, Mr. R. J. | 29.10.90 | Page, Mr. C. J. | 1. 6.94 |
| Garton, Mr. J. E. | 1. 1.91 | Robson, Mr. P. | 24. 2.95 |
| Wilcock, Mr. J. | 1. 1.91 | Gilmour, Mr. S. | 27.12.95 |
| Grantham, Mr. M. | 1. 8.91 | Turner Miss. S. R. | 19. 1.96 |
| Massey, Mr. P. J. | 1. 8.91 | Taylor, Mr. J. | 1. 4.96 |
| Robinson, Mr. J. | 1. 8.91 | Gittus, Miss C. L. | 14. 5.96 |
| Banister, Mr. N. | 28. 1.93 | Peasgood, Mr. D. J. | 14. 5.96 |
| North, Mr. Ashley | 16. 2.93 | Pepper, Mr. M. P. | 14. 5.96 |
| Barugh, Miss C. | 1. 6.93 | Wilkinson, Mr. P. | 10. 8.96 |
| Barugh, Miss H. | 1. 6.93 | Taylor, Mr. M. | 20. 8.96 |
| Turner, Mr. P. | 1.11.93 | Leggott, Mr. E. J. | 29. 8.96 |
| Atkins, Mr. J. | 24.12.93 | Lelke, Miss D. J. | 10.10.96 |
| Binley, Mr. R. J. | 24.12.93 | Canova, Mr. A. D. | 24.10.96 |
| Mortimer, Mr. Andrew | 24.12.93 | Wray, Mr. G. | 29.10.96 |
| Mortimer, Mr. P. | 24.12.93 | | |

# AUTOGRAPHS

# AUTOGRAPHS

# AUTOGRAPHS

# AUTOGRAPHS

# AUTOGRAPHS